MW00467389

QUOTE ME

QUOTE ME

WORLD'S MOST INSPIRING WORDS

Compiled
By Uplifting Publications

TABLE OF CONTENTS

Word from the Publisher:

It is the Publisher's desire that everyone can walk a little taller, carrying others who are down trodden and weary until they can walk a little taller as well. Not as one full of arrogance but one full of self-confidence and pride. Pride in oneself, family, friends, country, and with that pride rise up and take responsibility for things around them. The publisher takes on the view of the "The Optimist Clubs of America" and requests others to try and implement a little more love and a little less anger; to be a builder and not a destroyer; to up-lift those around them, and not bring them down.

"Let no corrupt communication proceed out of your mouth, but that which is good to the use of edifying, that it may minister grace unto the hearers." Ephesians 4:29

In many ways life is just to short to be lazy, shy, scared, mean, prideful, uncaring, angry, unloving and unlovable ect… so promise yourself the following:

-Promise Yourself-
To be so strong that nothing can disturb your peace of mind.
To talk health, happiness, and prosperity to every person you meet.
To make all your friends feel that there is something in them.
To look at the sunny side of everything and make your optimism come true.
To think only the best, to work only for the best and expect only the best.
To be just as enthusiastic about the success of others as you are about your own.
To forget the mistakes of the past and press on to the greater achievements of the future.
To give so much time to the improvement of yourself that you have no time to criticize others.
To be too large for worry, too noble for anger, too strong for fear, and too happy to permit the presence of trouble
-The Optimist Clubs Of America-

PART 1

Famous People:

I. Abraham Lincoln

It is better to remain silent and be thought a fool than to open one's mouth and remove all doubt.

Whatever you are, be a good one.

And in the end it is not the years in your life that count, it's the life in your years.

Nearly all men can stand adversity, but if you want to test a man's character, give him power.

How many legs does a dog have if you call the tail a leg? Four. Calling a tail a leg doesn't make it a leg.

Always bear in mind that your own resolution to success is more important than any other one thing.

Am I not destroying my enemies when I make friends of them.

Character is like a tree and reputation its shadow. The shadow is what we think it is; the tree is the real thing.

He has the right to criticize who has the heart to help.

I don't think much of a man who is not wiser today than he was yesterday.

It is difficult to make a man miserable while he feels worthy of himself and claims kindred to the great God who made him.

Nearly all men can stand adversity, but if you want to test a man's character, give him power.

Every man is said to have his peculiar ambition.

I am not bound to win, but I am bound to be true. I am not bound to succeed, but I am bound to live up to what light I have.

If you look for the worst in people and expect to find it, you surely will.

Let us have faith that right makes might, and that in faith, let us, to the end, dare to do our duty as we understand it.

People are just about as happy as they make up their minds to be.

That some should be rich, shows that others may become rich, and, hence, is just encouragement to industry and enterprise.

We should be too big to take offense and too noble to give it.

Be sure you put your feet in the right place, then stand firm.

All that I am or ever hope to be, I owe to my angel mother.

It has been my experience that folks who have no vices have very few virtues.

The Best thing about the future is that it comes one day at a time.

I will prepare and some day my chance will come.

Fourscore and seven years ago our fathers brought forth on this continent, a new nation, conceived in Liberty, and dedicated to the proposition that all men are created equal.

It's not me who can't keep a secret. It's the people I tell that can't.

Success is going from failure to failure without losing your enthusiasm.

I am a slow walker, but I never walk back.

Die when I may, I want it said by those who knew me best, that I always plucked a thistle and planted a flower where I thought a flower would grow.

Character is like a tree and reputation like its shadow. The shadow is what we think of it; the tree is the real thing.

A drop of honey catches more flies than a gallon of gall."

If you want to gather honey don't kick over the beehive

Always bear in mind that your own resolution to succeed is more important than any other thing.

Things may come to those who wait, but only the things left by those who hustle.

You cannot strengthen the weak by weakening the strong. You cannot help small men by tearing down big men. You cannot help the poor by destroying the rich. You cannot lift the wage earner by pulling down the wage-payer. You cannot keep out of trouble by spending more than your income. You cannot further the brotherhood of man by inciting class hatreds. You cannot build character and courage by taking away a man's initiative and independence. You cannot help men permanently by doing for them what they could and should do for themselves.

Always bear in mind that your own resolution to succeed is more important than any one thing.

Discourage litigation. Persuade your neighbors to compromise whenever you can. As a peacemaker the lawyer has superior opportunity of being a good man. There will still be business enough.

Force is all-conquering, but its victories are short-lived.

He can compress the most words into the smallest ideas of any man I ever met.

I am a firm believer in the people. If given the truth, they can be depended upon to meet any national crises. The great point is to bring them the real facts.

I will prepare and some day my chance will come.

If I were two-faced, would I be wearing this one?

If this is coffee, please bring me some tea; but if this is tea, please bring me some coffee.

If you would win a man to your cause, first convince him that you are his sincere friend.

It has been my experience that folks who have no vices have very few virtues.

It is difficult to make a man miserable while he feels worthy of himself and claims kindred to the great God who made him.

Let me not be understood as saying that there are no bad laws, nor that grievances may not arise for the redress of which no legal provisions have been made. I mean to say no such thing. But I do mean to say that although bad laws, if they exist, should be repealed as soon as possible, still, while they continue in force, for the sake of example they should be religiously observed.

Most folks are about as happy as they make up their minds to be.

Nearly all men can stand adversity, but if you want to test a man's character, give him power.

No man has a good enough memory to make a successful liar.

No man is good enough to govern another man without that other's consent.

Tact is the ability to describe others as they see themselves.

That some should be rich, shows that others may become rich, and, hence, is just encouragement to industry and enterprise.

The probability that we may fail in the struggle ought not to deter us from the support of a cause we believe to be just.

Whatever you are, be a good one.

When the conduct of men is designed to be influenced, persuasion, kind unassuming persuasion, should ever be adopted. It is an old and true maxim that 'a drop of honey catches more flies than a gallon of gall.' So with men. If you would win a man to your cause, first convince him that you are his sincere friend. Therein is a drop of honey that catches his heart, which, say what he will, is the great highroad to his reason, and which, once gained, you will find but little trouble in convincing him of the justice of your cause, if indeed that cause is really a good one.

When you have got an elephant by the hind leg, and he is trying to run away, it's best to let him run.

Whenever I hear anyone arguing for slavery, I feel a strong impulse to see it tried on him personally.

You cannot escape the responsibility of tomorrow by evading it today.

You may deceive all the people part of the time, and part of the people all the time, but not all the people all the time.

'Tis better to be silent and be thought a fool, than to speak and remove all doubt.

When I do good, I feel good; when I do bad, I feel bad, and that is my religion.

You can fool some of the people all of the time, and all of the people some of the time, but you can not fool all of the people all of the time.

II. Albert Einstein

Logic will get you from A to Z; imagination will get you everywhere.

If you want your children to be intelligent, read them fairy tales. If you want them to be more intelligent, read them more fairy tales.

I have no special talents. I am only passionately curious.

Two things are infinite: the universe and human stupidity; and I'm not sure about the universe.

Insanity: Doing the same thing over and over again and expecting different results.
The idle man does not know what it is to enjoy rest.

Time is relative; its only worth depends upon what we do as it is passing.

I am enough of an artist to draw freely upon my imagination. Imagination is more important than knowledge. Knowledge is limited. Imagination encircles the world.

Logic will get you from A to Z; imagination will get you everywhere.

When you are courting a nice girl an hour seems like a second. When you sit on a red-hot cinder a second seems like an hour. That's relativity.

Anyone who has never made a mistake has never tried anything new.

Education is what remains after one has forgotten what one has learned in school.

If you can't explain it to a six year old, you don't understand it yourself.

A clever person solves a problem. A wise person avoids it.

Learn from yesterday, live for today, hope for tomorrow. The important thing is to not stop questioning.

Try not to become a man of success. Rather become a man of value.

I know not with what weapons World War III will be fought, but World War IV will be fought with sticks and stones.

Life is like riding a bicycle. To keep your balance, you must keep moving.

If a cluttered desk is that of a cluttered mind, of what, then, is an empty desk?

Only a life lived for others is a life worthwhile.

Not everything that can be counted counts, and not everything that counts can be counted

III. Benjamin Franklin

Either write something worth reading or do something worth writing.

The definition of insanity is doing the same thing over and over and expecting different results.

Well done is better than well said.

By failing to prepare, you are preparing to fail.

Dost thou love life? Then do not squander time, for that's the stuff life is made of.

An investment in knowledge pays the best interest.

Early to bed and early to rise makes a man healthy, wealthy, and wise.

Instead of cursing the darkness, light a candle.

Never confuse Motion with Action. A slip of the foot you may soon recover, but a slip of the tongue you may never get over.

You may delay, but time will not.

Many people die at twenty five and aren't buried until they are seventy five.

Being ignorant is not so much a shame, as being unwilling to learn.

All mankind is divided into three classes: those that are immovable, those that are movable, and those that move.

All the little money that ever came into my hands was ever laid out in books.

Lost time is never found again

Happiness depends more on the inward disposition of mind than on outward circumstances.

While we may not be able to control all that happens to us, we can control what happens inside us.

You may delay, but time will not.

Dost thou love life? Then do not squander time for that's the stuff life is made of. He that is good for making excuses is seldom good for anything else.

Keep your eyes wide open before marriage, half shut afterwards.

An apple a day keeps the doctor away.

Never leave that till tomorrow what you can do today.

Speak ill of no man, but speak all the good you know of everybody.

Reading makes a full man, meditation a profound man, discourse a clear man.

He that speaks much, is much mistaken.

Words may show a man's wit, actions his meaning.

Whatever you become be good at it.

A house is not a home unless it contains food and fire for the mind as well as the body.

I wake up every morning at nine and grab for the morning paper. Then I look at the obituary page. If my name is not on it, I get up.

A good example is the best sermon.

In reality there is perhaps no one of our natural Passions so hard to subdue as Pride. Disguise it, struggle with it, beat it down, stifle it, mortify it as much as one pleases, it is still alive, and will now and then peek out and show itself.

It takes many good deeds to build a good reputation, and only one bad one to lose it.

If you would be loved, love, and be loveable.

IV. Buddha

Your work is to discover your world and then with all your heart give yourself to it.

All that we are is the result of what we have thought

The mind is everything; what you think, you become.

You will not be punished for your anger, you will be punished by your anger... Let a person overcome anger by love.

Hate is never ended be hatred but by love.

Believe nothing, no matter where you read it, or who said it, even if I have said it - unless it agrees with your own reason and your own common sense.

If you knew what I know about the power of giving, you would not let a single meal pass without sharing it in some way.

The thought manifests as the word;
The word manifests as the deed;
The deed develops into habit;
And habit hardens into character;
So watch the thought and its ways with care,
And let it spring from love
Born out of concern for all beings…
As the shadow follows the body,
As we think, so we become.

Hatred does not cease in this world by hating, but by not hating; this is an eternal truth.

V. C.S. Lewis

Love anything and your heart will be wrung and possibly broken. If you want to make sure of keeping it intact you must give it to no one, not even an animal. Wrap it carefully round with hobbies and little luxuries; avoid all entanglements. Lock it up safe in the casket or coffin of your selfishness. But in that casket, safe, dark, motionless, airless, it will change. It will not be broken; it will become unbreakable, impenetrable, irredeemable. To love is to be vulnerable.

Imagine yourself as a living house. God comes in to rebuild that house. At first, perhaps, you can understand what He is doing. He is getting the drains right and stopping the leaks in the roof and so on; you knew that those jobs needed doing and so you are not surprised. But presently He starts knocking the house about in a way that hurts abominably and does not seem to make any sense. What on earth is He up to? The explanation is that He is building quite a different house from the one you thought of - throwing out a new wing here, putting on an extra floor there, running up towers, making courtyards. You thought you were being made into a decent little cottage: but He is building a palace. He intends to come and live in it Himself.

The task of the modern educator is not to cut down jungles, but to irrigate deserts.

The homemaker has the ultimate career. All other careers exist for one purpose only and that is to support the ultimate career.

Why love if losing hurts so much? We love to know that we are not alone.

I can't imagine a man really enjoying a book and reading it only once.

A man can no more diminish God's glory by refusing to worship Him than a lunatic can put out the sun by scribbling the word 'darkness' on the walls of his cell.

Aim at heaven and you will get earth thrown in. Aim at earth and you get neither.

Can a mortal ask questions which God finds unanswerable? Quite easily, I should think. All nonsense questions are unanswerable.

Courage is not simply one of the virtues, but the form of every virtue at the testing point.

Do not let us mistake necessary evils for good.

Don't use words too big for the subject. Don't say 'infinitely' when you mean 'very'; otherwise you'll have no word left when you want to talk about something really infinite.

Education without values, as useful as it is, seems rather to make man a more clever devil.

Eros will have naked bodies; Friendship naked personalities.

Even in literature and art, no man who bothers about originality will ever be original: whereas if you simply try to tell the truth (without caring twopence how often it has been told before) you will, nine times out of ten, become original without ever having noticed it.

Failures are finger posts on the road to achievement.

Friendship is born at that moment when one person says to another: What! You too? I thought I was the only one.

If you look for truth, you may find comfort in the end; if you look for comfort you will not get either comfort or truth only soft soap and wishful thinking to begin, and in the end, despair.

It is hard to have patience with people who say "There is no death" or "Death doesn't matter." There is death. And whatever is matters. And whatever happens has consequences, and it and they are irrevocable and irreversible. You might as well say that birth doesn't matter.

It's so much easier to pray for a bore than to go and see one.

Of all tyrannies, a tyranny sincerely exercised for the good of its victims may be the most oppressive. It would be better to live under robber barons than under omnipotent moral busybodies. The robber baron's cruelty may sometimes sleep, his cupidity may at some point be satiated; but those who torment us for our own good will torment us without end for they do so with the approval of their own conscience.

The trouble about trying to make yourself stupider than you really are is that you very often succeed.

There are only two kinds of people in the end: those who say to God, 'Thy will be done,' and those to whom God says, in the end, 'Thy will be done.'

Mortal lovers must not try to remain at the first step; for lasting passion is the dream of a harlot and from it we wake in despair.

Every poem can be considered in two ways--as what the poet has to say, and as a thing which he makes.

Affection is responsible for nine-tenths of whatever solid and durable happiness there is in our lives.

If we discover a desire within us that nothing in this world can satisfy, also we should begin to wonder if perhaps we were created for another world.

No Christian and, indeed, no historian could accept the epigram which defines religion as 'what a man does with his solitude.'

VI. Dale Carnegie

You can make more friends in two months by becoming really interested in other people than you can in two years by trying to get other people interested in you.

People rarely succeed unless they have fun in what they are doing.

One of the most tragic things I know about human nature is that all of us tend to put off living. We are all dreaming of some magical rose garden over the horizon, instead of enjoying the roses that are blooming outside our windows today.

If you can't sleep, then get up and do something instead of lying there worrying. It's the worry that gets you, not the lack of sleep

When we hate our enemies, we are giving them power over us: power over our sleep, our appetites, our blood pressure, our health and our happiness. Our enemies would dance with joy if only they knew how they were worrying us, lacerating us, and getting even with us! Our hate is not hurting them at all, but our hate is turning our days and nights into a hellish turmoil.

Take a chance! All life is a chance. The man who goes furthest is generally the one who is willing to do and dare. The "sure thing" boat never gets far from shore.

Much of the best work of the world has been done against seeming impossibilities.

Are you bored with life? Then throw yourself into some work you believe in with all your heart, live for it, die for it, and you will find happiness that you had thought could never be yours.

Did you ever see an unhappy horse? Did you ever see a bird that had the blues? One reason why birds and horses are not unhappy is because they are not trying to impress other birds and horses.

VII. Edgar Allen Poe

Sound loves to revel in a summer night.

All that we see or seem, Is but a dream within a dream.

Years of love have been forgot, In the hatred of a minute.

To the glory that was Greece, And the grandeur that was Rome.

From a proud tower in the town, Death looks gigantically down.

Take thy beak from out my heart, and take thy form from off my door!

This maiden she lived with no other thought, Than to love and be loved by me.

And my soul from out that shadow that lies floating on the floor, Shall be lifted--Nevermore!

Can it be fancied that Deity ever vindictively, Made in his image a manikin merely to madden it?

I would define, in brief, the Poetry of words as the Rhythmical Creation of Beauty. Its sole arbiter is Taste.

Ah, distinctly I remember it was in the bleak December; And each separate dying ember wrought its ghost upon the floor.

And the silken, sad, uncertain rustling of each purple curtain, Thrilled me -- filled me with fantastic terrors never felt before.

Deep into that darkness peering, long I stood there, wondering, fearing, Doubting, dreaming dreams no mortal ever dreamed before.

Keeping time, time, time, In a sort of Runic rhyme, To the tintinnabulation that so musically wells, From the bells, bells, bells.

Hear the mellow wedding bells, Golden bells! What a world of happiness their harmony foretells, Through the balmy air of night, How they ring out their delight!

And all my days are trances, And all my nightly dreams, Are where thy dark eye glances, And where thy footstep gleams --iIn what ethereal dances, By what eternal streams.

The skies they were ashen and sober; the leaves they were crisped and serene. The leaves they were withering and sere; It was night in the lonesome October, Of my most immemorial year.

The object, Truth, or the satisfaction of the intellect, and the object, Passion, or the excitement of the heart, are, although attainable, to a certain extent, in poetry, far more readily attainable in prose.

VIII. Edmund Burke

Applaud us when we run, console us when we fall, cheer us when we recover.

If we command our wealth, we shall be rich and free. If our wealth commands us, we are poor indeed.

If you can be well without health, you may be happy without virtue.

No passion so effectually robs the mind of its powers of acting and reasoning as fear.

Our patience will achieve more than our force.

There is a boundary to men's passions when they act from feelings; but none when they are under the influence of imagination.

IX. Eleanor Roosevelt

Happiness is not a goal, it is a by-product.

I believe that anyone can conquer fear by doing the things he fears to do.

The most important thing in any relationship is not what you get but what you give. In any case, the giving of love is an education in itself.

It is not fair to ask of others what you are unwilling to do yourself.

It takes as much energy to wish as it does to plan.

People grow through experience if they meet life honestly and courageously. This is how character is built.

The purpose of life, after all, is to live it, to taste experience to the utmost, to reach out eagerly and without fear for newer and richer experiences.

We must want for others, not ourselves alone.

No one can make you feel inferior without your consent

With the new day comes new strength and new thoughts.

You gain strength, courage, and confidence by every experience in which you really stop to look fear in the face.

Do what you feel in your heart to be right- for you'll be criticized anyway. You'll be damned if you do, and damned if you don't.

You must do the thing you think you cannot do.

A woman is like a tea bag- you never know how strong she is until she gets in hot water.

Beautiful young people are accidents of nature, but beautiful old people are works of art.

Do what you feel in your heart to be right for you'll be criticized anyway. You'll be damned if you do, and damned if you don't.

Friendship with oneself is all-important, because without it one cannot be friends with anyone else in the world.

Great minds discuss ideas; Average minds discuss events; Small minds discuss people.

I could not at any age be content to take my place in a corner by the fireside and simply look on.

I think that somehow, we learn who we really are and then live with that decision.

If someone betrays you once, it's their fault; if they betray you twice, it's your fault.

It is not fair to ask of others what you are unwilling to do yourself.

Justice cannot be for one side alone, but must be for both.

Learn from the mistakes of others. You can't live long enough to make them all yourself.

Life was meant to be lived, and curiosity must be kept alive. One must never, for whatever reason, turn his back on life.

One thing life has taught me: if you are interested, you never have to look for new interests. They come to you. When you are genuinely interested in one thing, it will always lead to something else.

The purpose of life is to live it, to taste experience to the utmost, to reach out eagerly and without fear for newer and richer experience.

You gain strength, courage and confidence by every experience in which you really stop to look fear in the face. You are able to say to yourself, 'I have lived through this horror. I can take the next thing that comes along.' You must do the thing you think you cannot do.

People grow through experience if they meet life honestly and courageously. This is how character is built.

X. Emily Dickerson

A wounded deer leaps the highest.

Behavior is what a man does, not what he thinks, feels, or believes.

Fame is a fickle food upon a shifting plate.

Fortune befriends the bold.

Beauty is not caused. It is.

Anger as soon as fed is dead. 'Tis starving makes it fat.

Hope is the thing with feathers that perches in the soul.

My friends are my estate.

Success is counted sweetest by those who ne'er succeed.

They say that God is everywhere, and yet we always think of Him as somewhat of a recluse.

Love is anterior to life, posterior to death, initial of creation, and the exponent of breath.

Unable are the loved to die, for love is immortality.

Parting is all we know of heaven, and all we need of hell.

That it will never come again is what makes life sweet.

I do not like the man who squanders life for fame; give me the man who living makes a name.

To live is so startling it leaves little time for anything else.

Dying is a wild night and a new road.

The mere sense of living is joy enough.

Luck is not chance, it's toil; fortune's expensive smile is earned.

The brain is wider than the sky.

XI. Franklin D. Roosevelt

The only thing to fear is fear itself.

We may not be able to prepare the future for our children, but we can at least prepare our children for the future.

Books cannot be killed by fire. People die, but books never die. No man and no force can abolish memory... In this war, we know, books are weapons. And it is a part of your dedication always to make them weapons for man's freedom.

I'm not the smartest fellow in the world, but I can sure pick smart colleagues.

Great power involves great responsibility

It is common sense to take a method and try it. If it fails, admit it frankly and try another. But above all, try something.

The only limit to our realization of tomorrow will be our doubts of today.

In the truest sense freedom cannot be bestowed, it must be achieved.

When you get to the end of your rope, tie a knot and hang on.

As Americans, we go forward, in the service of our country, by the will of God.

Be sincere; be brief; be seated.

Happiness lies in the joy of achievement and the thrill of creative effort.

I sometimes think that the saving grace of America lies in the fact that the overwhelming majority of Americans are possessed of two great qualities- a sense of humor and a sense of proportion.

If you treat people right they will treat you right --ninety percent of the time.

It is common sense to take a method and try it. If it fails, admit it frankly and try another. But above all, try something.

The only limit to our realization of tomorrow will be our doubts of today. Let us move forward with strong and active faith.

The test of our progress is not whether we add more to the abundance of those who have much; it is whether we provide enough for those who have too little.

We cannot always build the future for our youth, but we can build our youth for the future.

We must remember that any oppression, any injustice, any hatred, is a wedge designed to attack our civilization.

Yesterday, December 7, 1941 -- a date which will live on in infamy -- the United States of America was suddenly and deliberately attacked by naval and air forces of the Empire of Japan.

First of all, let me assert my firm belief that the only thing we have to fear is fear itself -- nameless, unreasoning, unjustified terror which paralyzes needed efforts to convert retreat into advance.

It is fun to be in the same decade with you.

The only limit to our realization of tomorrow will be our doubts of today.

Men are not prisoners of fate, but only prisoners of their own minds.

When you get to the end of your rope, tie a knot and hang on.

A conservative is a man with two perfectly good legs who, however, has never learned to walk forward.

Repetition does not transform a lie into a truth.

The true conservative is the man who has a real concern for injustices and takes thought against the day of reckoning.

In the truest sense, freedom cannot be bestowed; it must be achieved.

XII. Gandi

As human beings, our greatness lies not so much in being able to remake the world -- that is the myth of the atomic age -- as in being able to remake ourselves.

Be the change you want to see in the world.

First they ignore you, then they laugh at you, then they fight you, then you win.

God is conscience. He is even the atheism of the atheist.

Honest disagreement is often a good sign of progress.

If by strength is meant moral power, then woman is immeasurably man's superior.

No power on earth can subjugate you when you are armed with the sword of ahimsa. It ennobles both the victor and the vanquished.

Nobody can hurt me without my permission.

There is more to life than simply increasing its speed.

XIII. G.K. Chesterton

Fairy tales, are more than true. Not because they tell us that dragons exist, but because they tell us that dragons can be defeated.

Just going to church doesn't make you a Christian any more than standing in your garage makes you a car.

There are two ways to get enough. One is to continue to accumulate more and more. The other is to desire less.

There are no uninteresting things, only uninterested people.

If there were no God, there would be no atheists.

The Bible tells us to love our neighbors, and also to love our enemies; probably because generally they are the same people.

The way to love anything is to realize that it might be lost.

XIV. Gordon B. Hinckley

Life is to be enjoyed, not endured

If Life Gets Too Hard To Stand, Kneel.

You have not failed until you quit trying.

Stop seeking out the storms and enjoy more fully the sunlight.

If we could follow the slogan that says, “Turn off the TV and open a good book" we would do something of substance for a future generation.

You can't plow a field simply by turning it over in your mind.

Without hard work, nothing grows but weeds.

Forget yourself and get to work.

There is something almost sacred about a great library because it represents the preservation of the wisdom, the learning, and the pondering of men and women of all the ages, accumulated under one roof.

There is something wonderful about a book. We can pick it up. We can heft it. We can read it. We can set it down. We can think of what we have read. It does something for us. We can share great minds, great actions, and great undertakings in the pages of a book.

It is not so much the major events as the small day-to-day decisions that map the course of our living. . . Our lives are, in reality, the sum total of our seemingly unimportant decisions and of our capacity to live by those decisions.

The greatness of the world in which we live is the accumulated goodness of many small and seemingly inconsequential acts.

Love is like the North Star. In a changing world, it's always constant.

Being humble means recognizing that we are not on earth to see how important we can become, but to see how much difference we can make in the lives of others.

Do the best you can. But I want to emphasize that it be the very best. We are too prone to be satisfied with mediocre performance. We are capable of doing so much better.

The best antidote I know for worry is work. The best medicine for despair is service. The best cure for weariness is the challenge of helping someone who is even more tired.

That which comes easily departs easily. That which comes of struggle remains.

Work is the miracle by which talent is brought to the surface and dreams become reality.

The cause of most of man's unhappiness is sacrificing what he wants most for what he wants now.

Love is meant to be an adventure!

I know of no other practice which will make one more attractive in conversation than to be well-read in a variety of subjects. There is a great potential within each of us to go on learning. Regardless of our age, unless there be serious illness, we can read, study, drink in the writings of wonderful men and women. It is never too late to learn.

Knowledge without labor is profitless. Knowledge with labor is genius.

Things will work out. Keep trying. Be believing. Don't get discouraged. Things will work out.

XV. Henry David Thoreau

Goodness is the only investment which never fails.

Dreams are the touchstones of our character.

It's not what you look at that matters, it's what you see.

Do not be too moral. You may cheat yourself out of much life so. Aim above morality. Be not simply good, be good for something.

Read the best books first, or you may not have a chance to read them at all.

There is no remedy for love, but to love more.

Men profess to be lovers of music, but for the most part they give no evidence in their opinions and lives that they have heard it.

Happiness is like a butterfly. The more you chase it, the more it will elude you; but if you turn your attention to other things, it will come and sit softly on your shoulder.

Dreams are the touchstones of our characters.

As if you could kill time without injuring eternity

...be yourself, not your idea of what you think somebody else's idea of yourself should be.

How many a man has dated a new era in his life from the reading of a book.

One is not born into the world to do everything but to do something.

The greatest compliment that was ever paid me was when one asked me what I thought, and attended to my answer.

If one advances confidently in the direction of his dreams, and endeavors to live the life which he has imagined, he will meet with a success unexpected in common hours.

Go confidently in the direction of your dreams! Live the life you've imagined. As you simplify your life, the laws of the universe will be simpler.

Success usually comes to those who are too busy to be looking for it.

Do not hire a man who does your work for money, but him who does it for love of it

Men are born to succeed, not to fail.

Only that day dawns to which we are awake.

A man is rich in proportion to the number of things he can afford to let alone.

Public opinion is a weak tyrant compared with our own private opinion. What a man thinks of himself, that is which determines, or rather indicates, his fate.

Rather than love, than money, than fame, give me truth.

Some circumstantial evidence is very strong, as when you find a trout in the milk.

Success usually comes to those who are too busy to be looking for it.

Thank God men cannot as yet fly and lay waste the sky as well as the earth!

That man is the richest whose pleasures are the cheapest.

The character inherent in the American people has done all that has been accomplished; and it would have done somewhat more, if the government had not sometimes got in its way.

The cost of a thing is the amount of what I call life which is required to be exchanged for it, immediately or in the long run.

To regret deeply is to live afresh.

Under a government which imprisons any unjustly, the true place for a just man is in prison.

We must have infinite faith in each other. If we have not, we must never let it leak out that we have not.

What is the use of a house if you haven't got a tolerable planet to put it on?

What people say you cannot do, you try and find that you can.

When a dog runs at you, whistle for him.

[Water is] the only drink for a wise man.

Every generation laughs at the old fashions, but follows religiously the new.

The mass of men lead lives of quiet desperation.

It is never too late to give up our prejudices.

But government in which the majority rule in all cases can not be based on justice, even as far as men understand it.

He enjoys true leisure who has time to improve his soul's estate.

Man is the artificer of his own happiness.

There is no remedy for love but to love more.

Beware of all enterprises that require new clothes.

Our inventions are wont to be pretty toys, which distract our attention from serious things. They are but improved means to an unimproved end.

When we are unhurried and wise, we perceive that only great and worthy things have any permanent and absolute existence, that petty fears and petty pleasures are but the shadow of the reality.

I went to the woods because I wished to live deliberately, to front only the essential facts of life, and see if I could not learn what it had to teach, and not, when I came to die, discover that I had not lived.

Things do not change; we change.

I say beware of all enterprises that require new clothes, and not rather a new wearer of clothes.

It is an interesting question how far men would retain their relative rank if they were divested of their clothes.

The finest qualities of our nature, like the bloom on fruits, can be preserved only by the most delicate handling. Yet we do not treat ourselves nor one another thus tenderly.

Any fool can make a rule, and any fool will mind it.

As if you could kill time without injuring eternity.

Be true to your work, your word, and your friend.

Books are the carriers of civilization. Without books, history is silent, literature dumb, science crippled, thought and speculation at a standstill. I think that there is nothing, not even crime, more opposed to poetry, to philosophy, ay, to life itself than this incessant business.

Cultivate the habit of early rising. It is unwise to keep the head long on a level with the feet.

Do not be too moral. You may cheat yourself out of much life. Aim above morality. Be not simply good; be good for something.

Do not hire a man who does your work for money, but him who does it for love of it.

Every man is the builder of a temple called his body.

Go confidently in the direction of your dreams! Live the life you've imagined. As you simplify your life, the laws of the universe will be simpler.

He enjoys true leisure who has time to improve his soul's estate.

How vain it is to sit down to write when you have not stood up to live.

However mean your life is, meet it and live it: do not shun it and call it hard names. Cultivate poverty like a garden herb, like sage. Do not trouble yourself much to get new things, whether clothes or friends. Things do not change, we change. Sell your clothes and keep your thoughts. God will see that you do want society.

I know of no more encouraging fact than the unquestioned ability of a man to elevate his life by conscious endeavor.

I once had a sparrow alight upon my shoulder for a moment, while I was hoeing in a village garden, and I felt that I was more distinguished by that circumstance that I should have been by any epaulet I could have worn.

I stand in awe of my body.

If one advances confidently in the direction of his dreams, and endeavors to live the life which he has imagined, he will meet with a success unexpected in common hours.

If you have built castles in the air, your work need not be lost; that is where they should be. Now put the foundations under them.

If you would convince a man that he does wrong, do right. But do not care to convince him. Men will believe what they see. Let them see.

If you would convince a man that he does wrong, do right. Men will believe what they see.

In what concerns you much, do not think that you have companions: know that you are alone in the world.

In wildness is the preservation of the world.

It is as hard to see one's self as to look backwards without turning around.

It is never too late to give up your prejudices.

Live each season as it passes; breathe the air, drink the drink, taste the fruit, and resign yourself to the influences of each.

Men are born to succeed, not fail.

Men have become the tools of their tools.

Most are engaged in business the greater part of their lives, because the soul abhors a vacuum and they have not discovered any continuous employment for man's nobler faculties.

My friend is one... who take me for what I am.

Our life is frittered away by detail. Simplify, simplify.

XVI. James Allen

A man is literally what he thinks, his character being the complete sum of all his thoughts.

Cherish your visions. Cherish your ideals. Cherish the music that stirs in your heart, the beauty that forms in your mind, the loveliness that drapes your purest thoughts, for out of them will grow all delightful conditions, all heavenly environment, of these, if you but remain true to them your world will at last be built.

The soul attracts that which it secretly harbors, that which it loves, and also that which it fears. It reaches the height of its cherished aspirations. It falls to the level of its unchastened desires - and circumstances are the means by which the soul receives its own.

Every action and feeling is preceded by a thought.

Right thinking begins with the words we say to ourselves.

If anything is excellent or praiseworthy, think about such things.

XVII. Marcus Aelius Aurelius

It is not death that a man should fear, but he should fear never beginning to live.

If you are distressed by anything external, the pain is not due to the thing itself but to your own estimate of it; and this you have the power to revoke at any moment.

If you are distressed by anything external, the pain is not due to the thing itself but to your own estimate of it; and this you have the power to revoke at any moment.

The soul is dyed the color of it's thoughts

The true worth of a man is to be measured by the objects he pursues.

How much time he saves who does not look to see what his neighbor says or does or thinks.

If you are distressed by anything external, the pain is not due to the thing itself, but to your estimate of it; and this you have the power to revoke at any moment.

If you are pained by external things, it is not they that disturb you, but your own judgment of them. And it is in your power to wipe out that judgment now.

It is the act of a madman to pursue impossibilities.

Look well into thyself; there is a source of strength which will always spring up if thou wilt always look there.

Remember this, that there is a proper dignity and proportion to be observed in the performance of every act of life.

The happiness of your life depends upon the quality of your thoughts, therefore guard accordingly; and take care that you entertain no notions unsuitable to virtue, and reasonable nature.

Waste no more time talking about great souls and how they should be. Become one yourself!

By a tranquil mind I mean nothing else than a mind well ordered.

How much time he gains who does not look to see what his neighbor says or does or thinks, but only at what he does himself, to make it just and holy.

In the morning, when you are sluggish about getting up, let this thought be present: 'I am rising to a man's work.'

Never esteem anything as of advantage to you that will make you break your word or lose your self-respect.

Nothing happens to any thing which that thing is not made by nature to bear.

Nothing happens to anybody which he is not fitted by nature to bear.

The universe is change; our life is what our thoughts make it.

Think not disdainfully of death, but look on it with favor; for even death is one of the things that Nature wills.

Very little is needed to make a happy life.

Whatever is in any way beautiful hath its source of beauty in itself, and is complete in itself; praise forms no part of it. So it is none the worse nor the better for being praised.

You will find rest from vain fancies if you perform every act in life as though it were your last.

Never let the future disturb you. You will meet it, if you have to, with the same weapons of reason which today arm you against the present.

XVIII. Mark twain

There are several good protections against temptation, but the surest is cowardice.

One of the striking differences between a cat and a lie is that a cat has only nine lives.

The holy passion of Friendship is of so sweet and steady and loyal and enduring a nature that it will last through a whole lifetime, if not asked to lend money.

Clothes make the man. Naked people have little or no influence in society.

Let us be thankful for the fools. But for them the rest of us could not succeed.

It's not the size of the dog in the fight, it's the size of the fight in the dog.

The man who does not read good books has no advantage over the man who can't read them.

Wrinkles should merely indicate where smiles have been.

The only way to keep your health is to eat what you don't want, drink what you don't like, and do what you'd rather not.

Let us endeavor to live so that when we come to die even the undertaker will be sorry.

The fear of death follows from the fear of life. A man who lives fully is prepared to die at any time.

Never put off until tomorrow what you can do the day after tomorrow.

XIX. Martin Luther King Jr.

Faith is taking the first step even when you can't see the whole staircase.

We must build dikes of courage to hold back the flood of fear.

If I wish to compose or write or pray or preach well, I must be angry. Then all the blood in my veins is stirred, and my understanding is sharpened.

In the end, we will remember not the words of our enemies, but the silence of our friends.

The ultimate measure of a man is not where he stands in moments of comfort and convenience, but where he stands at times of challenge and controversy.

Intelligence plus character-that is the goal of true education.

If you can't fly then run, if you can't run then walk, if you can't walk then crawl, but whatever you do you have to keep moving forward.

If a man is called to be a street sweeper, he should sweep streets even as a Michaelangelo painted, or Beethoven composed music or Shakespeare wrote poetry. He should sweep streets so well that all the hosts of heaven and earth will pause to say, here lived a great street sweeper who did his job well.

Nothing in the world is more dangerous than sincere ignorance and conscientious stupidity.

On some positions, Cowardice asks the question, "Is it safe?" Expediency asks the question, "Is it politic?" And Vanity comes along and asks the question, "Is it popular?" But Conscience asks the question "Is it right?" And there comes a time when one must take a position that is neither safe, nor politic, nor popular, but he must do it because Conscience tells him it is right.

Those who are not looking for happiness are the most likely to find it, because those who are searching forget that the surest way to be happy is to seek happiness for others.

I have a dream that one day people will be judged not by the color of their skin but by the content of their character.

People fail to get along because they fear each other; they fear each other because they don't know each other; they don't know each other because they have not communicated with each other.

The time is always right to do the right thing

Only in the darkness can you see the stars.

An individual has not started living until he can rise above the narrow confines of his individualistic concerns to the broader concerns of all humanity.

Science investigates; religion interprets. Science gives man knowledge, which is power; religion gives man wisdom, which is control. Science deals mainly with facts; religion deals mainly with values. The two are not rivals.

Life's most persistent and urgent question is, 'What are you doing for others?

Everyone has the power for greatness—not for fame, but greatness, because greatness is determined by service.

Every man must decide whether he will walk in the light of creative altruism or in the darkness of destructive selfishness.

The quality, not the longevity, of one's life is what is important.

No work is insignificant. All labor that uplifts humanity has dignity and importance and should be undertaken with painstaking excellence.

Morality cannot be legislated, but behavior can be regulated. Judicial decrees may not change the heart, but they can restrain the heartless.

A genuine leader is not a searcher for consensus but a molder of consensus.

We must use time creatively - and forever realize that the time is always hope to do great things.

We must remember that intelligence is not enough. Intelligence plus character that is the goal of true education. The complete education gives one not only power of concentration, but worthy objectives upon which to concentrate.

The soft-minded man always fears change. He feels security in the status quo, and he has an almost morbid fear of the new. For him, the greatest pain is the pain of a new idea.

If a man hasn't discovered something he will die for, he isn't fit to live.

A man who won't die for something is not fit to live.

We are now faced with the fact that tomorrow is today. We are confronted with the fierce urgency of now. In this unfolding conundrum of life and history, there "is" such a thing as being too late. This is no time for apathy or complacency. This is a time for vigorous and positive action.

If physical death is the price that I must pay to free my white brothers and sisters from a permanent death of the spirit, then nothing can be more redemptive.

Injustice anywhere is a threat to justice everywhere.

A genuine leader is not a searcher for consensus but a molder of consensus.

A lie cannot live.

A man can't ride your back unless it's bent.

A nation or civilization that continues to produce soft-minded men purchases its own spiritual death on the installment plan.

A nation that continues year after year to spend more money on military defense than on programs of social uplift is approaching spiritual doom.

All progress is precarious, and the solution of one problem brings us face to face with another problem.

Almost always, the creative dedicated minority has made the world better.

We will speed the day when all of God's children, black men and white men, Jews and Gentiles, Protestants and Catholics, will be able to join hands and sing... Free at last, free at last, thank God Almighty, I'm free at last.

Before the Pilgrims landed at Plymouth, we were here. Before the pen of Jefferson etched across the pages of history the majestic words of the Declaration of Independence, we were here. If the inexpressible cruelties of slavery could not stop us, the opposition we now face will surely fail.

Darkness cannot drive out darkness; only light can do that. Hate cannot drive out hate; only love can do that.

Discrimination is a hellhound that gnaws at Negroes in every waking moment of their lives to remind them that the lie of their inferiority is accepted as truth in the society dominating them.

A right delayed is a right denied.

A riot is at bottom the language of the unheard.

All labor that uplifts humanity has dignity and importance and should be undertaken with painstaking excellence.

An individual who breaks a law that conscience tells him is unjust, and who willingly accepts the penalty of imprisonment in order to arouse the conscience of the community over its injustice, is in reality expressing the highest respect for the law.

At the center of non-violence stands the principle of love.

Every man must decide whether he will walk in the light of creative altruism or in the darkness of destructive selfishness.

Everybody can be great, because anybody can serve. You don't have to have a college degree to serve. You don't have to make your subject and verb agree to serve. You only need a heart full of grace. A soul generated by love.

Everything that we see is a shadow cast by that which we do not see.

Man must evolve for all human conflict a method which rejects revenge, aggression and retaliation. The foundation of such a method is love.

Nonviolence is absolute commitment to the way of love. Love is not emotional bash; it is not empty sentimentalism. It is the active outpouring of one's whole being into the being of another.

Our lives begin to end the day we become silent about things that matter.

Our nettlesome task is to discover how to organize our strength into compelling power.

The good neighbor looks beyond the external accidents and discerns those inner qualities that make all men human and, therefore, brothers.

Faith is taking the first step even when you don't see the whole staircase.

Freedom is never voluntarily given by the oppressor; it must be demanded by the oppressed.

The sweltering summer of the Negro's legitimate discontent will not pass until there is an invigorating autumn of freedom and equality.

The ultimate test of a man is not where he stands in moments of comfort and moments of convenience, but where he stands in moments of challenge and moments of controversy.

There are two types of laws; there are just laws and there are unjust laws... What is the difference between the two? An unjust law is a man-made code that is out of harmony with the moral law.

I refuse to accept the cynical notion that nation after nation must spiral down a militaristic stairway into the hell of nuclear annihilation... I believe that even amid today's mortar bursts and whining bullets, there is still hope for a brighter tomorrow... I still believe that one day mankind will bow before the altars of God and be crowned triumphant over war and bloodshed.

XX. Michelangelo.

Faith in one's self... is the best and safest course.

Genius is eternal patience.

I saw the angel in the marble and carved until I set him free.

The greater danger for most of us is not that our aim is too high and we miss it, but that it is too low and we hit it.

The marble not yet carved can hold the form of every thought the greatest artist has.

The true work of art is but a shadow of the divine perfection.

XXI. Nelson Mandela

True reconciliation does not consist in merely forgetting the past.

Only free men can negotiate; prisoners cannot enter into contracts.

Education is the most powerful weapon, which you can use to change the world.

Extremists on all sides thrive, fed by the blood lust of centuries gone by.

As we are liberated from our own fear, our presence automatically liberates others.

There is no such thing as part freedom.

For to be free is not merely to cast off one's chains, but to live in a way that respects and enhances the freedom of others.

A good head and a good heart are always a formidable combination.

As we are liberated from our own fear, our presence automatically liberates others.

If you want to make peace with your enemy, you have to work with your enemy. Then he becomes your partner.

I cannot conceive of Israel withdrawing if Arab states do not recognize Israel, within secure borders.

We must use time wisely and forever realize that the time is always ripe to do right.

When the water starts boiling it is foolish to turn off the heat.

I learned that courage was not the absence of fear, but the triumph over it. The brave man is not he who does not feel afraid, but he who conquers that fear.

I dream of an Africa which is in peace with itself.

In my country we go to prison first and then become President.

Man's goodness is a flame that can be hidden but never extinguished.

I am not a saint, unless you think of a saint as a sinner who keeps on trying.

XXII. Nietzsche

I was in darkness, but I took three steps and found myself in paradise. The first step was a good thought, the second, a good word; and the third, a good deed.

Many are stubborn in pursuit of the path they have chosen, few in pursuit of the goal.

It is not a lack of love, but a lack of friendship that makes unhappy marriages

When one has a great deal to put into it a day has a hundred pockets.

Battle not with monsters, lest ye become a monster, and if you gaze into the abyss, the abyss gazes also into you.

Be careful when you fight the monsters, lest you become one.

In truth, there was only one Christian, and he died on the cross.

Insanity in individuals is something rare, but in groups, parties, nations and epochs, it is the rule.

It is hard enough to remember my opinions, without also remembering my reasons for them!

No price is too high to pay for the privilege of owning yourself.

One must have a good memory to be able to keep the promises one makes.

Talking much about oneself can also be a means to conceal oneself.

The advantage of a bad memory is that one enjoys several times the same good things for the first time.

The individual has always had to struggle to keep from being overwhelmed by the tribe. If you try it, you will be lonely often, and sometimes frightened. But no price is too high to pay for the privilege of owning yourself.

The irrationality of a thing is no argument against its existence, rather a condition of it.

The overman...Who has organized the chaos of his passions, given style to his character, and become creative. Aware of life's terrors, he affirms life without resentment.

The visionary lies to himself, the liar only to others.

To forget one's purpose is the commonest form of stupidity.

To predict the behavior of ordinary people in advance, you only have to assume that they will always try to escape a disagreeable situation with the smallest possible expenditure of intelligence.

What else is love but understanding and rejoicing in the fact that another person lives, acts, and experiences otherwise than we do…?

When one has much to put into them, a day has a hundred pockets.

When you stare into the abyss the abyss stares back at you.

You need chaos in your soul to give birth to a dancing star.

There is always some madness in love. But there is also always some reason in madness.

But thus do I counsel you, my friends: distrust all in whom the impulse to punish is powerful!

Digressions, objections, delight in mockery, carefree mistrust are signs of health; everything unconditional belongs in pathology.

Poets are shameless with their experiences: they exploit them.

He who fights with monsters might take care lest he thereby become a monster. And if you gaze for long into an abyss, the abyss gazes also into you.

What is done out of love always takes place beyond good and evil.

Only sick music makes money today.

The man of knowledge must be able not only to love his enemies but also to hate his friends.

What is good? All that heightens the feeling of power in man, the will to power, power itself. What is bad? All that is born of weakness. What is happiness? The feeling that power is growing, that resistance is overcome.

The surest way to corrupt a youth is to instruct him to hold in higher esteem those who think alike than those who think differently.

Morality is herd instinct in the individual.

To find everything profound that is an inconvenient trait. It makes one strain one's eyes all the time, and in the end one finds more than one might have wished.

We are always in our own company.

The most perfidious way of harming a cause consists of defending it deliberately with faulty arguments.

For believe me: the secret for harvesting from existence the greatest fruitfulness and greatest enjoyment is to live dangerously.

I would not know what the spirit of a philosopher might wish more to be than a good dancer.

A thinker sees his own actions as experiments and questions--as attempts to find out something. Success and failure are for him answers above all.

Out of life's school of war: What does not destroy me, makes me stronger.

For men are not equal: thus speaks justice.

I am a law only for my kind, I am no law for all.

It is nobler to declare oneself wrong than to insist on being right - especially when one is right.

Not by wrath does one kill, but by laughter.

What does not kill me, makes me stronger.

XXIII. Norman Vincent Peale

The one person who most blocks you from a full, happy, and successful life is you. He is therefore wise who makes himself an asset. We can be our own worst enemy or best friend. We can be a source of trouble or a cure for trouble. So if you feel empty, as many do, start by getting free from yourself as a first stop to vibrant living.

Think excitement, talk excitement, act out excitement, and you are bound to become an excited person. Life will take on a new zest, deeper interest and greater meaning. You can think, talk and act yourself into dullness or into monotony or into unhappiness. By the same process you can build up inspiration, excitement and surging depth of joy.

The greatest measure of human being isn't how he handles himself when things are going well, but how he handles himself when things are going badly, when defeat comes.

The mind, properly controlled, can do just about everything. You can think your way through adversity, you can think your way through problems. It is a super powerful instrument which so few use to maximum. And if the mind thinks with a believing attitude one can do amazing things.

Empty pockets never held anyone back. Only empty heads and empty hearts can do that.

The man who lives for himself is a failure; the man who lives for others has achieved true success.

There is a real magic in enthusiasm. It spells the difference between mediocrity and accomplishment... It gives warmth and good feeling to all your personal relationships.

XIV. PLATO

Be kind, for everyone you meet is fighting a hard battle.

Death is not the worst that can happen to men.

If women are expected to do the same work as men, we must teach them the same things.

Ignorance, the root and the stem of every evil.

Laws are partly formed for the sake of good men, in order to instruct them how they may live on friendly terms with one another, and partly for the sake of those who refuse to be instructed, whose spirit cannot be subdued, or softened, or hindered from plunging into evil.

Man...is a tame or civilized animal; never the less, he requires proper instruction and a fortunate nature, and then of all animals he becomes the most divine and most civilized; but if he be insufficiently or ill-educated he is the most savage of earthly creatures.

Never discourage anyone... who continually makes progress, no matter how slow.

Never discourage anyone...who continually makes progress, no matter how slow.

No human thing is of serious importance.

Only the dead have seen the end of war.

The price good men pay for indifference to public affairs is to be ruled by evil men.

There is no such thing as a lover's oath.

They certainly give very strange names to diseases.

We can easily forgive a child who is afraid of the dark; the real tragedy of life is when men are afraid of the light.

Wise men talk because they have something to say; fools, because they have to say something.

You can discover more about a person in an hour of play than in a year of conversation.

No evil can happen to a good man, either in life or after death.

You cannot conceive the many without the one.

False words are not only evil in themselves, but they infect the soul with evil.

Must not all things at the last be swallowed up in death?

I have hardly ever known a mathematician who was capable of reasoning.

Mankind censure injustice fearing that they may be the victims of it, and not because they shrink from committing it.

Necessity, who is the mother of invention.

The beginning is the most important part of the work.

The direction in which education starts a man will determine his future life.

The people have always some champion whom they set over them and nurse into greatness...This and no other is the root from which a tyrant springs; when he first appears he is a protector.

The soul of man is immortal and imperishable.

There are three arts which are concerned with all things: one which uses, another which makes, and a third which imitates them.

Wealth is the parent of luxury and indolence, and poverty of meanness and viciousness, and both of discontent.

When there is an income tax, the just man will pay more and the unjust less on the same amount of income.

The partisan, when he is engaged in a dispute, cares nothing about the rights of the question, but is anxious only to convince his hearers of his own assertions.

Friends have all things in common.

The greatest penalty of evil doing is namely, to grow into the likeness of bad men.

You are young, my son, and, as the years go by, time will change and even reverse many of your present opinions. Refrain therefore awhile from setting yourself up as a judge of the highest matters.

Any one who has common sense will remember that the bewilderments of the eyes are of two kinds, and arise from two causes, either from coming out of the light or from going into the light, which is true of the mind's eye, quite as much as of the bodily eye; and he who remembers this when he sees any one whose vision is perplexed and weak, will not be too ready to laugh; he will first ask whether that soul of man has come out of the brighter light, and is unable to see because unaccustomed to the dark, or having turned from darkness to the day is dazzled by excess of light.

Astronomy compels the soul to look upwards and leads us from this world to another.

Bodily exercise, when compulsory, does no harm to the body; but knowledge which is acquired under compulsion obtains no hold on the mind.

Everything that deceives may be said to enchant.

He who is of calm and happy nature will hardly feel the pressure of age, but to him who is of an opposite disposition youth and age are equally a burden.

XXV. Ralph Waldo Emerson

The glory of friendship is not the outstretched hand, nor the kindly smile, nor the joy of companionship; it's the spiritual inspiration that comes to one when he discovers that someone else believes in him and is willing to trust him with his friendship

Wherever you are, be there.

A man is what he thinks about all day long.

A hero is a man who is afraid to run away.

Imagination is not a talent of some men but is the health of every man."

To believe your own thought, to believe that what is true for you in your private heart is true for all men, - that is genius.

What lies behind us and lies before us are small matters compared to what lies within us.

To be yourself in a world that is constantly trying to make you something else is the greatest accomplishment.

For every minute you are angry you lose sixty seconds of happiness.

We are always getting ready to live but never living.

Always do what you are afraid to do.

Those are a success who have lived well, laughed often, and loved much; who have gained the respect of intelligent people and the love of children, who have filled their niche and accomplished their task, who leave the world better than they found it, whether by a perfect poem or a rescued soul; who never lacked appreciation of the earth's beauty or failed to express it; who looked for the best in others and gave the best they had.

What you do speaks so loudly that I cannot hear what you say.

When it is dark enough, you can see the stars.

Do not go where the path may lead, go instead where there is no path and leave a trail.

Our greatest glory is not in never failing, but in rising up every time we fail.

The reward of a thing well done is to have done it.

Do not be too timid and squeamish about your actions. All life is an experiment. The more experiments you make the better. What if they are a little course and you may get your coat soiled or torn? What if you do fail, and get fairly rolled in the dirt once or twice. Up again, you shall never be so afraid of a tumble.

There is no limit to what can be accomplished if it doesn't matter who gets the credit.

Guard well your spare moments. They are like uncut diamonds. Discard them and their value will never be known. Improve them and they will become the brightest gems in a useful life.

Fear defeats more people than any other one thing in the world.

It is not the length of life, but the depth.

It is easy in the world to live after the world's opinion; it is easy in solitude to live after our own; but the great man is he who in the midst of the crowd keeps with perfect sweetness the independence of solitude."

Don't be too timid and squeamish about your actions. All life is an experiment. The more experiments you make the better.

You cannot do a kindness too soon, for you never know how soon it will be too late.

Make the most of yourself...for that is all there is of you.

Once you make a decision, the universe conspires to make it happen.

The only way to have a friend is to be one.

Dare to live the life you have dreamed for yourself. Go forward and make your dreams come true.

All I have seen teaches me to trust the Creator for all I have not seen.

If we encounter a man of rare intellect, we should ask him what books he reads.

Life is a journey, not a destination.

Guard well your spare moments. They are like uncut diamonds. Discard them and their value will never be known. Improve them and they will become the brightest gems in a useful life.

Every artist was first an amateur.

That which we persist in doing becomes easier to do, not that the nature of the thing has changed but that our power to do has increased.

Without ambition one starts nothing. Without work one finishes nothing. The prize will not be sent to you. You have to win it.

Though we travel the world over to find the beautiful, we must carry it with us or we find it not.

Nothing is more sacred than the integrity of your own mind.

Every man I meet is my superior in some way. In that, I learn of him.

An individual has a healthy personality to the exact degree to which they have the propensity to look for the good in every situation.

So much of our time is preparation, so much is routine, and so much retrospect, that the path of each man's genius contracts itself to a very few hours.

A friend is one before whom I may think aloud.

A hero is no braver than an ordinary man, but he is braver five minutes longer.

A man of genius is privileged only as far as he is genius. His dullness is as insupportable as any other dullness.

All I have seen teaches me to trust the Creator for all I have not seen.

All our progress is an unfolding, like a vegetable bud. You have first an instinct, then an opinion, then a knowledge as the plant has root, bud, and fruit. Trust the instinct to the end, though you can render no reason.

As we grow old… the beauty steals inward.

Be not the slave of your own past. Plunge into the sublime seas, dive deep and swim far, so you shall come back with self-respect, with new power, with an advanced experience that shall explain and overlook the old.

Beware when the great God lets loose a thinker on this planet.

Character is higher than intellect... A great soul will be strong to live, as well as to think.

Children are all foreigners.

Colleges hate geniuses, just as convents hate saints.

Conversation is an art in which a man has all mankind for his competitors, for it is that which all are practising every day while they live.

Democracy becomes a government of bullies tempered by editors.

Do not go where the path may lead, go instead where there is no path and leave a trail.

Don't be too timid and squeamish about your actions. All life is an experiment. The more experiments you make the better.

Don't waste yourself in rejection, nor bark against the bad, but chant the beauty of the good.

Every great and commanding moment in the annals of the world is the triumph of some enthusiasm.

Every hero becomes a bore at last.

Every sweet has its sour; every evil its good.

Finish each day and be done with it. You have done what you could.

Give all to love; obey thy heart.

God enters by a private door into every individual.

He has not learned the lesson of life who does not every day surmount a fear.

I awoke this morning with devout thanksgiving for my friends, the old and the new.

I hate quotations. Tell me what you know.

I pack my trunk, embrace my friends, embark on the sea, and at last wake up in Naples, and there beside me is the Stern Fact, the Sad Self, unrelenting, identical, that I fled from.

If I have lost confidence in myself, I have the universe against me.

Insist on yourself; never imitate... Every great man is unique.

Let not a man guard his dignity, but let his dignity guard him.

Live in the sunshine, swim the sea, drink the wild air…

Make the most of yourself, for that is all there is of you.

Make yourself necessary to somebody. Do not make life hard to any.

Money, which represents the prose of life, and which is hardly spoken of in parlors without an apology, is, in its effects and laws, as beautiful as roses.

Nature magically suits a man to his fortunes, by making them the fruit of his character.

No great man ever complains of want of opportunity.

None of us will ever accomplish anything excellent or commanding except when he listens to this whisper which is heard by him alone.

Nothing can bring you peace but yourself.

Nothing great was ever achieved without enthusiasm.

Nothing is at last sacred but the integrity of your own mind.

Our chief want in life is somebody who shall make us do what we can.

Our knowledge is the amassed thought and experience of innumerable minds.

People seem not to see that their opinion of the world is also a confession of their character.

Shallow men believe in luck. Strong men believe in cause and effect.

That which we persist in doing becomes easier, not that the task itself has become easier, but that our ability to perform it has improved.

The adventitious beauty of poetry may be felt in the greater delight with a verse given in a happy quotation than in the poem.

The ancestor of every action is a thought.

The end of the human race will be that it will eventually die of civilization.

The essence of all jokes, of all comedy, seems to be an honest or well intended halfness; a non performance of that which is pretended to be performed, at the same time that one is giving loud pledges of performance. The balking of the intellect, is comedy and it announces itself in the pleasant spasms we call laughter.

The key to every man is his thought. Sturdy and defying though he look, he has a helm which he obeys, which is the idea after which all his facts are classified. He can only be reformed by showing him a new idea which commands his own.

The life of man is the true romance, which when it is valiantly conduced, will yield the imagination a higher joy than any fiction.

The louder he talked of his honor, the faster we counted our spoons.

The measure of a master is his success in bringing all men around to his opinion twenty years later.

The only gift is a portion of thyself.

The only way to have a friend is to be one.

The ornament of a house is the friends who frequent it.

The peril of every fine faculty is the delight of playing with it for pride. Talent is commonly developed at the expense of character, and the greater it grows, the more is the mischief. Talent is mistaken for genius, a dogma or system for truth, ambition for greatest, ingenuity for poetry, sensuality for art.

The world belongs to the energetic.

There are many things of which a wise man might wish to be ignorant.

There is no den in the wide world to hide a rogue. Commit a crime and the earth is made of glass. Commit a crime, and it seems as if a coat of snow fell on the ground, such as reveals in the woods the track of every partridge, and fox, and squirrel.

This time, like all times, is a very good one, if we but know what to do with it.

Those who cannot tell what they desire or expect, still sigh and struggle with indefinite thoughts and vast wishes.

Write it on your heart that every day is the best day in the year. No man has learned anything rightly, until he knows that every day is Doomsday.

Tis the good reader that makes the good book.

Trust your instinct to the end, though you can render no reason.

Truth is beautiful, without doubt; but so are lies.

We all boil at different degrees.

We do what we must, and call it by the best names.

What you do speaks so loud that I cannot hear what you say.

When you strike at a king, you must kill him.

Whoever is open, loyal, true; of humane and affable demeanour; honourable himself, and in his judgement of others; faithful to his word as to law, and faithful alike to God and man....such a man is a true gentleman.

Whoso would be a man must be a nonconformist.

Work and acquire, and thou hast chained the wheel of Chance.

Hitch your wagon to a star.

In every work of genius we recognize our own rejected thoughts; they come back to us with a certain alienated majesty.

Speak what you think today in hard words and tomorrow speak what tomorrow thinks in hard words again, though it contradict every thing you said today.

Nothing astonishes men so much as common sense and plain dealing.

Sometimes a scream is better than a thesis.

Finish each day and be done with it. You have done what you could. Some blunders and absurdities no doubt crept in; forget them as soon as you can. Tomorrow is a new day; begin it well and serenely and with too high a spirit to be encumbered with your old nonsense.

What lies behind us and what lies before us are tiny matters compared to what lies within us.

He who is in love is wise and is becoming wiser, sees newly every time he looks at the object beloved, drawing from it with his eyes and his mind those virtues which it possesses.

To be great is to be misunderstood.

Trust men and they will be true to you; treat them greatly, and they will show themselves great.

Immortality. I notice that as soon as writers broach this question they begin to quote. I hate quotation. Tell me what you know.

When a whole nation is roaring Patriotism at the top of its voice, I am fain to explore the cleanness of its hands and purity of its heart.

The best effect of fine persons is felt after we have left their presence.

Next to the originator of a good sentence is the first quoter of it.

Every artist was first an amateur.

In the highest civilization, the book is still the highest delight. He who has once known its satisfactions is provided with a resource against calamity.

Wit makes its own welcome, and levels all distinctions. No dignity, no learning, no force of character, can make any stand against good wit.

The bitterest tragic element in life to be derived from an intellectual source is the belief in a brute Fate or Destiny.

Men are conservatives when they are least vigorous, or when they are most luxurious. They are conservatives after dinner.

In every work of genius we see our own rejected thoughts.

It is easy in the world to live after the world's opinion; it is easy in solitude to live after our own; but the great man is he who in the midst of the crowd keeps with perfect sweetness the independence of solitude.

A foolish consistency is the hobgoblin of little minds, adored by little statesmen and philosophers and divines.

As soon as there is life there is danger.

A man builds a fine house; and now he has a master, and a task for life; he is to furnish, watch, show it, and keep it in repair, the rest of his days.

The reward of a thing well done is to have done it.

XXVI. Rudyard Kipling

Asia is not going to be civilized after the methods of the West. There is too much Asia and she is too old.

Power without responsibility, the prerogative of the harlot throughout the ages.

For the strength of the Pack is the Wolf, and the strength of the Wolf is the Pack.

The silliest woman can manage a clever man; but it needs a clever woman to manage a fool.

Words are, of course, the most powerful drug used by mankind.

The first condition of understanding a foreign country is to smell it.

I always prefer to believe the best of everybody, it saves so much trouble.

Gardens are not made by singing "Oh, how beautiful," and sitting in the shade.

I keep six honest serving-men (They taught me all I knew); Their names are What and Why and When And How and Where and Who.

Borrow trouble for yourself, if that's your nature, but don't lend it to your neighbors.

If you can keep your head when all about you
Are losing theirs and blaming it on you.

Too much work and too much energy kill a man just as effectively as too much assorted vice or too much drink.

Fill the unforgiving minute with sixty seconds worth of distance run.

XXVII. Sir Winston Churchill

We make a living by what we get, but we make a life by what we give.

A pessimist sees the difficulty in every opportunity; an optimist sees the opportunity in every difficulty.

It is no use saying, 'We are doing our best.' You have got to succeed in doing what is necessary. If you are going through hell, keep going.

You have enemies? Good. That means you've stood up for something, sometime in your life.

Those that fail to learn from history, are doomed to repeat it.

We are masters of the unsaid words, but slaves of those we let slip out.

The price of greatness is responsibility.

Kites rise highest against the wind, not with it.

Those that fail to learn from history, are doomed to repeat it.

It is a good thing for an uneducated man to read books of quotations. If you have an important point to make, don't try to be subtle or clever. Use a pile driver. Hit the point once. Then come back and hit it again. Then hit it a third time a tremendous whack.

The farther backwards you can look, the farther forward you are likely to see.

Courage is what it takes to stand up and speak. Courage is also what it takes to sit down and listen.

There is no doubt that it is around the family and the home that all the greatest virtues, the most dominating virtues of human, are created, strengthened and maintained.

I have nothing to offer but blood, toil, tears and sweat.

History is written by the victors.

To each there comes in their lifetime a special moment when they are figuratively tapped on the shoulder and offered the chance to do a very special thing, unique to them and fitted to their talents. What a tragedy if that moment finds them unprepared or unqualified for that which could have been their finest hour.

Success is not final, failure is not fatal: it is the courage to continue that counts.

Success is going from failure to failure without a loss of enthusiasm.

Success is never final.

Responsibility is the price of greatness.

The price of greatness is responsibility.

Attitude is a little thing that makes a big difference.

To each there comes in their lifetime a special moment when they are figuratively tapped on the shoulder and offered the chance to do a very special thing, unique to them and fitted to their talents. What a tragedy if that moment finds them unprepared or unqualified for that which could have been their finest hour.

XXVIII. Thomas Paine

Character is much easier kept than recovered.

I love the man that can smile in trouble, that can gather strength from distress, and grow brave by reflection.

It is necessary to the happiness of man that he be mentally faithful to himself.

Reputation is what men and women think of us; character is what God and angels know of us.

The harder the conflict, the more glorious the triumph.

The real man smiles in trouble, gathers strength from distress, and grows brave by reflection.

We have it in our power to begin the world over again.

What we obtain too cheap we esteem too little; it is dearness only that gives everything value.

XXIX. Wilde

Always forgive your enemies; nothing annoys them so much.

A little sincerity is a dangerous thing, and a great deal of it is absolutely fatal.

Anyone who lives within their means suffers from a lack of imagination.

Biography lends to death a new terror.

I am not young enough to know everything.

A cynic is a man who knows the price of everything but the value of nothing

A gentleman is one whonever hurts anyone's feelings unintentionally

A man who does not think for himself does not think at all.

A poet can survive everything but a misprint.

All art is quite useless.

Ordinary riches can be stolen, real riches cannot. In your soul are infinitely precious things that cannot be taken from you.

I have the simplest tastes. I am always satisfied with the best.

Man can believe the impossible, but can never believe the improbable.

Whenever a man does a thoroughly stupid thing, it is always from the noblest motives.

There are only two tragedies in life: one is not getting what one wants, and the other is getting it.

They spoil every romance by trying to make it last forever.

Experience is the name everyone gives to their mistakes.

Democracy means simply the bludgeoning of the people by the people for the people.

The only way to get rid of a temptation is to yield to it.

There is only one thing in the world worse than being talked about, and that is not being talked about.

XXX. William James

Be not afraid of life. Believe that life is worth living, and your belief will help create that fact.

The greatest discovery of my generation is that human beings can alter their lives by altering their attitudes of mind.

The greatest discovery of my generation is that human beings can alter their lives by altering their attitudes of mind.

Compared with what we ought to be, we are only half awake.

Your hopes, dreams and aspirations are legitimate. They are trying to take you airborne, above the clouds, above the storms, if you only let them.

There is no worse lie than a truth misunderstood by those who hear it.

A great many people think they are thinking when they are really rearranging their prejudices.

As a rule we disbelieve all the facts and theories for which we have no use.

Be not afraid of life. Believe that life is worth living, and your belief will help create the fact.

Human beings, by changing the inner attitudes of their minds, can change the outer aspects of their lives.

The art of being wise is the art of knowing what to overlook.

The greatest discovery of my generation is that a human being can alter his life by altering his attitudes of mind.

The greatest use of life is to spend it for something that will outlast it.

The stream of thought flows on; but most of its segments fall into the bottomless abyss of oblivion. Of some, no memory survives the instant of their passage. Of others, it is confined to a few moments, hours or days. Others, again, leave vestiges which are indestructible, and by means of which they may be recalled as long as life endures.

There is only one thing a philosopher can be relied upon to do, and that is to contradict other philosophers.

Whenever two people meet, there are really six people present. There is each man as he sees himself, each man as the other person sees him, and each man as he really is.

XXXI. William Shakespeare

We know what we are, but know not what we may be.

A fool thinks himself to be wise, but a wise man knows himself to be a fool.

Love looks not with the eyes, but with the mind.

There is nothing either good or bad but thinking makes it so.

Be not afraid of greatness; some are born great, some achieve greatness, and others have greatness thrust upon them.

I will praise any man that will praise me.

Don't trust the person who has broken faith once.

I wasted time, and now doth time waste me.

A wretched soul, bruised with adversity,
We bid be quiet when we hear it cry;
But were we burdened with like weight of pain,
As much or more we should ourselves complain.

Action is eloquence.

Cowards die many times before their deaths;
The valiant never taste of death but once.

And since you know you cannot see yourself,
so well as by reflection, I, your glass,
will modestly discover to yourself,
that of yourself which you yet know not of.

And thus I clothe my naked villainy
With old odd ends, stol'n forth of holy writ;
And seem a saint, when most I play the devil.

Assume a virtue, if you have it not.

Be great in act, as you have been in thought.

Blow, blow, thou winter wind
Thou art not so unkind,
As man's ingratitude.

Conversation should be pleasant without scurrility, witty without affectation, free without indecency, learned without conceitedness, novel without falsehood.

For they are yet ear-kissing arguments.

Free from gross passion or of mirth or anger
constant in spirit, not swerving with the blood,
garnish'd and deck'd in modest compliment,
not working with the eye without the ear,
and but in purged judgement trusting neither?
Such and so finely bolted didst thou seem.

Glory is like a circle in the water,
Which never ceaseth to enlarge itself,
Till by broad spreading it disperses to naught.

God bless thee; and put meekness in thy mind, love, charity, obedience, and true duty!

He who has injured thee was either stronger or weaker than thee. If weaker, spare him; if stronger, spare thyself.

His life was gentle; and the elements
So mixed in him, that Nature might stand up,
And say to all the world, THIS WAS A MAN!

How poor are they who have not patience! What wound did ever heal but by degrees.

How use doth breed a habit in a man.

I am not bound to please thee with my answers.

I did never know so full a voice issue from so empty a heart: but the saying is true 'The empty vessel makes the greatest sound'.

I dote on his very absence.

I feel within me a peace above all earthly dignities, a still and quiet conscience.

I hate ingratitude more in a man
than lying, vainness, babbling, drunkenness,
or any taint of vice whose strong corruption
inhabits our frail blood.

I must be cruel only to be kind;
Thus bad begins, and worse remains behind.

I pray thee cease thy counsel,
Which falls into mine ears as profitless
as water in a sieve.

I pray you bear me henceforth from the noise and rumour of the field, where I may think the remnant of my thoughts in peace, and part of this body and my soul with contemplation and devout desires.

I wish you well and so I take my leave,
I Pray you know me when we meet again.

Ill deeds are doubled with an evil word.

In a false quarrel there is no true valour.

In peace there's nothing so becomes a man as modest stillness and humility.

In time we hate that which we often fear.

XXXII. Winston Churchill

Never in the field of human conflict was so much owed by so many to so few.

I have nothing to offer but blood, toil, tears and sweat.

A fanatic is one who can't change his mind and won't change the subject.

The inherent vice of capitalism is the uneven division of blessings, while the inherent virtue of socialism is the equal division of misery.

It is no use saying, 'We are doing our best.' You have got to succeed in doing what is necessary.

Success is going from failure to failure without a loss of enthusiam.

The greatest lesson in life is to know that even fools are right sometimes.

He has all the virtues I dislike and none of the vices I admire.

The problems of victory are more agreeable than the problems of defeat, but they are no less difficult.

Democracy is the worst form of government except for all those others that have been tried.

A pessimist sees the difficulty in every opportunity; an optimist sees the opportunity in every difficulty.

It is no use saying, 'We are doing our best.' You have got to succeed in doing what is necessary.

Attitude is a little thing that makes a big difference.

If you are going through hell, keep going.

Success is not final, failure is not fatal: it is the courage to continue that counts.

To each there comes in their lifetime a special moment when they are figuratively tapped on the shoulder and offered the chance to do a very special thing, unique to them and fitted to their talents. What a tragedy if that moment finds them unprepared or unqualified for that which could have been their finest hour.

I have nothing to offer but blood, toil, tears and sweat.

XXXIII. Zig Ziglar

If standard of living is our major objective, quality of life almost never improves, but if quality of life is your number one objective, your standard of living almost always improves.

You will make a lousy anybody else, but you will be the best "you" in existence.

Motivation gets you going and habit gets you there. Make motivation a habit and you will get there more quickly and have more fun on the trip.

You cannot tailor make the situations in life, but you can tailor make the attitudes to fit those situations before they arise.

Other people and things can stop you temporarily. You're the only one who can do it permanently.

You are the only one who can use your ability. It is an awesome responsibility. It was character that got us out of bed, commitment that moved us into action, and discipline that enabled us to follow through.

When you choose to be pleasant and positive in the way you treat others, you have also chosen, in most cases, how you are going to be treated by them.

People often say that motivation doesn't last. Well, neither does bathing that's why we recommend it daily.

Motivation is the fuel necessary to keep the human engine running.

Don't be distracted by criticism. Remember the only taste of success some people have is when they take a bite out of you.

Failure is an event, not a person. Yesterday ended last night.

Success is the maximum utilization of the ability that you have.

The most practical, beautiful, workable philosophy in the world won't work if you won't.

Of all the attitudes we can acquire, surely the attitude of gratitude is the most important and by far the most life-changing.

You can get everything money will buy without a lick of character, but you can't get any of the things money won't buy happiness, joy, peace of mind, winning relationships, etc. without character

PART II

Theme Quotes

I. Attitude

A positive attitude is essential for a happy and fulfilled life. It's hard to find joy in any situation if ones attitude is dross. There is no situation in life where a bad attitude will make the situation better, but a good attitude will always help in the matter. It's not easy to always be positive. It's just like anything we do we must learn and learn, then put into practice. A positive attitude is no different. One must have the desire to have a good attitude and then work on it until it becomes a reality. It just doesn't come. One doesn't simple know how to be a cook just because they desire to cook. They must learn, try, make mistakes, and keep on trying and learning. It is only through commitment and work that one is able to make progress.

If you don't like something, change it. If you can't change it, change your attitude. Don't complain. ~Maya Angelou

Develop your willpower so that you can make yourself do what you should do, when you should do it, whether you feel like it or not. ~Brian Tracy

Life can get foggy, but I can always rise above it.~ Chris Sonognini

People are just about as happy as they make up their minds to be. ~ Abraham Lincoln

I am not bound to win, but I am bound to be true. I am not bound to succeed, but I am bound to live up to what light I have. ~Abraham Lincoln

If you look for the worst in people and expect to find it, you surely will. ~ Abraham Lincoln

It's not enough to be good if you have the ability to be better. ~Alberta Lee Cox

If you think you can, or you think you can't, you're right! ~Henry Ford

A happy person is not a person in a certain set of circumstances, but rather a person with a certain set of attitudes. ~Hugh Downs

There is no such thing as can't, only won't. If you're qualified, all it takes is a burning desire to accomplish, to make a change. Go forward, go backward. Whatever it takes. ~Jan Ashford

A pessimist sees the difficulty in every opportunity; an optimist sees the opportunity in every difficulty. ~Winston Churchhill

It is no use saying, 'We are doing our best.' You have got to succeed in doing what is necessary. ~Winston Churchill

I am convinced that attitude is the key to success or failure in almost any of life's endeavors. Your attitude - your perspective, your outlook, how you feel about yourself, how you feel about other people - determines your priorities, your actions, your values. Your attitude determines how you interact with other people and how you interact with yourself. ~Carolyn Warner

Man is made or unmade by himself; in the armory of thought he forges the weapons by which he destroys himself. He also fashions the tools with which he builds for himself heavenly mansions of joy and strength and peace. By the right choice and true application of thought, man ascends to the Divine Perfection; by the abuse and wrong application of thought, he descends below the level of the beast. Between these two extremes are all the grades of character, and man is their maker and master. ~James Allen

Attitude is a little thing that makes a big difference. ~Winston S. Churchill

Life is 10% what happens to you and 90% what you do with what happens to you! ~ Anonymous

Desire is the key to motivation, but it's determination and commitment to an unrelenting pursuit of your goal --a commitment to excellence --that will enable you to attain the success you seek. ~Mario Andretti

As a man Thinketh in his heart, so is he ~ David, the psalmist

A great attitude does much more than turn on the lights in our worlds, it seems to magically connect us to all sorts of serendipitous opportunities that were somehow absent before the change. ~Earl Nightingale

The greater part of our happiness or misery depends on our disposition and not our circumstances. ~Martha Washington

The mind, properly controlled, can do just about everything. You can think your way through adversity, you can think your way through problems. It is a super powerful instrument which so few use to maximum. And if the mind thinks with a believing attitude one can do amazing things. ~Norman Vincent Peale

No person who is enthusiastic about his work has anything to fear from life. All the opportunities in the world are waiting to be grasped by people who are in love with what they're doing. ~Samuel Goldwyn

They can because they think they can. ~Virgil

Life's battles don't always go to the stronger or faster man. But sooner or later the man who wins, is the man who thinks he can. ~Vince Lombardi

There's always the motivation of wanting to win. Everybody has that. But a champion needs, in his attitude, a motivation above and beyond winning. ~Pat Riley

Eccentricity is not, as dull people would have us believe, a form of madness. It is often a kind of innocent pride, and the man of genius and the aristocrat are frequently regarded as eccentrics because genius and aristocrat are entirely unafraid of and uninfluenced by the opinions and vagaries of the crowd. ~Edith Sitwell

A positive attitude may not solve all your problems, but it will annoy enough people to make it worth the effort. ~Herm Albright

I happen to feel that the degree of a person's intelligence is directly reflected by the number of conflicting attitudes she can bring to bear on the same topic. ~Lisa Alther,

Complaining is good for you as long as you're not complaining to the person you're complaining about. ~Lynn Johnston

I am still determined to be cheerful and happy, in whatever situation I may be; for I have also learned from experience that the greater part of our happiness or misery depends upon our dispositions, and not upon our circumstances. ~Martha Washington

A strong positive mental attitude will create more miracles than any wonder drug. ~ Patricia Neal

No one can make you feel inferior without your consent. ~Eleanor Roosevelt

So often we dwell on the things that seem impossible rather than on the things that are possible. So often we are depressed by what remains to be done and forget to be thankful for all that has been done. ~Marian Wright Edelman

Whenever you're in conflict with someone, there is one factor that can make the difference between damaging your relationship and deepening it. That factor is attitude. ~Timothy Bentley

You're not obligated to win. You're obligated to keep trying to do the best you can every day. ~Marian Wright Edelman

There is no such thing in anyone's life as an unimportant day. ~Alexander Woolcott

Never think of the consequences of failing, you will always think of a negative result. Think only positive thoughts and your mind will gravitate towards those thoughts! ~Michael Jordan

When people are highly motivated, it's easy to accomplish the impossible. And when they're not, it's impossible to accomplish the easy. ~Bob Collings

The secret of discipline is motivation. When a man is sufficiently motivated, discipline will take care of itself. ~Sir Alexander Paterson

Ability is what you're capable of doing. Motivation determines what you do. Attitude determines how well you do it. ~Lou Holtz

Enthusiasm is the element of success in everything. It is the light that leads and the strength that lifts people on and up in the great struggles of scientific pursuits and of professional labor. It robs endurance of difficulty, and makes pleasure of duty. ~Bishop Doane

Every memorable act in the history of the world is a triumph of enthusiasm. Nothing great was ever achieved without it because it gives any challenge or any occupation, no matter how frightening or difficult, a new meaning. Without enthusiasm you are doomed to a life of mediocrity but with it you can accomplish miracles. ~Og Mandino

Enthusiasm is the greatest asset in the world. It beats money and power and influence. ~Henry Chester

Any activity becomes creative when the doer cares about doing it right, or doing it better. ~John Updike

It's not the load that breaks you down, it's the way you carry it. ~Lena Horne

Don't waste your time trying to control the uncontrollable, or trying to solve the unsolvable, or think about what could have been. Instead, think about what you 'can' control and solve the problem you 'can' solve with the wisdom you have gained from both your victories and your defeats in the past. ~David Mahoney

Make a game of finding something positive in every situation. Ninety-five percent of your emotions are determined by how you interpret events to yourself. ~Brian Tracey

The attitudes of your friends are like the buttons on an elevator. They will either take you up or they will take you down. ~Alexander Lockhart

You can't always control the circumstances in life, but you can control your attitude toward those circumstances. ~Alexander Lockhart

A positive attitude is like a fire. Unless you continue to add fuel, it goes out. ~Alexander Lockhart

You cannot tailor make the situations in life, but you can tailor make the attitudes to fit those situations before they arise. ~Zig Ziglar

Other people and things can stop you temporarily. You're the only one who can do it permanently. ~Zig Ziglar

Don't be distracted by criticism. Remember ~the only taste of success some people have is when they take a bite out of you. ~Zig Ziglar

Motivation gets you going and habit gets you there. Make motivation a habit and you will get there more quickly and have more fun on the trip. ~Zig Ziglar

A positive attitude won't let you do anything. But it will let you do everything better than a negative attitude will. ~Zig Ziglar

Positive thinking will let you do everything better than negative thinking will. ~Zig Zigler

Everyone thinks of changing the world, but no one thinks of changing himself. ~Leo Tolstoy

If you want to be happy, be. ~Leo Tolstoy

Even though you may not be responsible for what happens to you, you are responsible for how you react to what happens to you - it's just a matter of how you control your attitude. ~unknown

You may not be responsible for being down, but you must be responsible for getting up. ~Jesse Jackson

Non-participation gives us hardening of the attitude. Life goes on, and if we do not participate, life still goes on. If a negative attitude is not getting us where we want to go, then why not change the attitude? Reshaping attitudes is possible. Awareness is the key initial step. ~Marsha Petrie Sue

The more anger towards the past you carry in your heart, the less capable you are of loving in the present. ~Barbara De Angelis

He who angers you conquers you. ~Elizabeth Kenny

No one else 'makes us angry.' We make ourselves angry when we surrender control of our attitude. What someone else may have done is irrelevant. We choose, not they. They merely put our attitude to a test. ~Jim Rohn

You will not be punished for your anger, you will be punished by your anger... Let a person overcome anger by love. ~Buddha

If you are patient in one moment of anger, you will escape a hundred days of sorrow. ~Chinese proverb

Confidence is contagious. So is lack of confidence. ~Vince Lombardi

If you aren't fired with enthusiasm, you will be fired with enthusiasm. ~Vince Lombardi

Never say that you have no time. On the whole it is those who are busiest who can make time for yet more, and those who love more leisure time who refused to do something when asked. What we lack is not time, but heart. ~Henri Boulard

Choose your friends carefully. A negative attitude is very contagious and can rub off on you little by little without your knowledge. ~Unknown

Attitudes are contagious is yours worth catching? ~Anonymous

A healthy attitude is contagious but don't wait to catch it from others. Be a carrier. ~Anonymous

Although at the moment they may be equal in their lack of a real answer, the man who replies I'll find out, is much more valuable to his employer, his neighbor, and to himself than the man who replies l don't know. ~Anonymous

Attitudes are contagious. Are yours worth catching? ~Anonymous

His mother asked him why he said that when the day was anything but beautiful. Mother, said he, with rare wisdom, never judge a day by its weather. ~Anonymous

I can alter my life by altering the attitude of my mind. –Anonymous

Sometimes we are limited more by attitude than by opportunities. –Anonymous

Take charge of your attitude. Don't let someone else choose it for you. ~Anonymous

The control center of your life is your attitude. ~Anonymous

Although fate presents the circumstances, how you react depends on your character. ~Anonymous

II. Be True to Thy Self

Perhaps there is nothing in life more important than to be true to "thine own self." Nothing brings more satisfaction and nothing can bring more heart ache. Our own conscience is a strict task maker. One can actually mute ones conscience to an extent where it can't be heard—that may be the most dangerous thing to anyone human. Without it one can never reach any state of happiness for they have fallen victims of apathy and disgruntlement. An attitude of, "I don't care" is the most dangerous of all, destructive in nature. It will destroy anyone. Thus, it is imperative to know 'thy self' in order to be truly content with oneself. It is good to know what our values and morals are. What we want to stand for. What we are not willing to stand for. Know our limits. Learn to recognize weakness, and have the desire to improve. When we know who we are, or who we want to be then we are able to live the life we want to live, and to always be true to ourselves.

This above all: to thine own self be true,
And it must follow, as the night the day,
Thou canst not then be false to any man.
~William Shakespeare

Happiness is when what you think, what you say, and what you do are in harmony. ~Mahatma Gandhi

In matters of conscience, the law of the majority has no place. ~Mahatma Gandhi

If you have integrity, nothing else matters. If you don't have integrity, nothing else matters. ~Alan Simpson

If a man does his best, what else is there? ~General George S. Patton

Do what you feel in your heart to be right- for you'll be criticized anyway. You'll be damned if you do, and damned if you don't. ~Eleanor Roosevelt

No bird soars too high if he soars with his own wings. ~William Blake

The time is always right to do what is right. ~Dr. Martin Luther King, Jr.

They're certainly entitled to think that, and they're entitled to full respect for their opinions, but before I can live with other folks I've got to live with myself. The one thing that doesn't abide by majority rule is a person's conscience. ~Harper Lee (Atticus)

I don't know the key to success, but the key to failure is trying to please everybody. ~Bill Cosby

Try not to become a man of success, but rather try to become a man of value. ~Albert Einstein

I should love to satisfy all, if I possibly can; but in trying to satisfy all, I may be able to satisfy none. I have, therefore, arrived at the conclusion that the best course is to satisfy one's own conscience and leave the world to form its own judgment, favorable or otherwise. ~Mohandas K. Gandhi

The goal of compassion is not to care because someone is like us but to care because they are themselves. ~Mary Lou Randour

To believe your own thought, to believe that what is true for you in your private heart is true for all men, -- that is genius. ~Ralph Waldo Emerson

Let the world know you as you are, not as you think you should be, because sooner or later, if you are posing, you will forget the pose, and then where are you? ~Fanny Brice

Always be a first-rate version of yourself, instead of a second-rate version of someone else. ~Judy Garland

You will make a lousy anybody else, but you will be the best "you" in existence. ~Zig Ziglar

In matters of conscience, the law of the majority has no place.~ Gandhi

Life's only limitations are those you set upon yourself, for as long as you strive hard enough anything is achievable. ~Chad Williams

Do you want to know who you are? Don't ask. Act! Action will delineate and define you. ~Thomas Jefferson

Words may show a man's wit, but actions his meaning. ~Benjamin Franklin

It is better to be hated for what you are than to be loved for what you are not. ~Andre Gide

When you are content to be simply yourself and don't compare or compete, everybody will respect you. ~Lao Tzu

Be who you are and say what you feel because those who mind don't matter and those who matter don't mind. ~Theodor Seuss Geisel, "Dr. Seuss”

The heart has its reasons which reason does not know. ~Blaise Pascal

The voice of conscience is so delicate that it is easy to stifle it; but it is also so clear that it is impossible to mistake it. ~Madame De Stael

What lies behind us and lies before us are small matters compared to what lies within us. ~Ralph Waldo Emerson

If you look into your own heart, and you find nothing wrong there, what is there to worry about? What is there to fear? ~Confucius

Failures are divided into two classes: Those who thought and never did, and those who did and never thought. ~John Charles Salak

Success is that peace of mind that comes from knowing you've done everything in your power to become the very best you're capable of becoming. ~John Wooden

Cowardice asks the question, "Is it safe?" Expediency asks the question, "Is it politic?" Vanity asks the question, "Is it popular?" But, conscience asks the question, "Is it right?" And there comes a time when one must take a position that is neither safe, nor politic, nor popular, but one must take it because one's conscience tells one that it is right. ~Dr. Martin Luther King, Jr.

Believe nothing, no matter where you read it, or who said it, even if I have said it - unless it agrees with your own reason and your own common sense. ~Buddha

One person of integrity can make a difference. ~Elie Wiesel

“The eye is the lamp of the body. So if your eye is sound, your whole body will be full of light; but if your eye is not sound, your whole body will be full of darkness.”~ Matt. 6: 22-23

At a distance from home a man is judged by what he means. ~Anonymous

Character is a diamond that scratches every other stone. ~Anonymous

Character is a victory, not a gift. ~Anonymous

Character, like a kettle, once mended, always requires repairs. ~Anonymous

It's not the work that's hard, it's the discipline. ~Anonymous

Reputation is the shell a man discards when he leaves life for immortality. His character he takes with him. ~Anonymous

Reputation is what the world thinks a man is; character is what he really is. ~Anonymous

Self-determination is fine but needs to be tempered with self-control. ~Anonymous

The true gentleman does not preach his beliefs until he does so by his actions. ~Anonymous

III. Finding Success

How does one find success in life? What is the definition of success? Do we use a definition of the world?—how big is my estate—or do we measure success personally? Does it really matter how much material things we have in life when we lay down to die, or is it more important to leave a positive legacy behind?

In order to find more success in life one needs to take advantage of opportunities. One can wait for opportunities to come along or go out of one's way and make opportunities. An English poet once wrote, "Come to the edge," He said."We can't, it's too high." "Come to the edge, "He said. "We can't, we might fall. "Come to the edge," He said. And they came. And he pushed, And they flew! In order to live life to its fullest one has to go out of his way, to put oneself in uncomfortable positions. One is more likely to grow and learn when they don't feel comfortable and content about a situation.

There are many paths to the top of the mountain, but only one view. ~Harry Millner

Success is a journey, not a destination. ~Ben Sweetland

In order to succeed, your desire for success should be greater than your fear of failure. ~Bill Cosby

Success is simple. Do what's right, the right way, at the right time. ~Arnold H. Glasow

The reward for work well done is the opportunity to do more. ~Jonas Salk

Each success only buys an admission ticket to a more difficult problem. ~Henry A. Kissinger

Success only breeds a new goal. ~Bette Davis

Success is never final. ~Winston Churchill

Success is a journey not a destination. The doing is usually more important than the outcome. Not everyone can be Number 1. ~Arthur Ashe

You've achieved success in your field when you don't know whether what you are doing is work or play. ~Warren Beatty

If winning isn't everything, why do they keep score? ~Vince Lombardi

Dictionary is the only place that success comes before work. Hard work is the price we must pay for success. I think you can accomplish anything if you're willing to pay the price. ~Vince Lombardi

Champions know there are Success is not a 'sometimes' thing. In other words, you don't do what is right once in awhile, but all the time. Success is a habit. Winning is a habit. ~Vincent Thomas Lombardi

Winning is not a sometime thing; it's an all-time thing. You don't win once in a while, you don't do things right once in a while, you do them all the time. Winning is a habit. ~Vince Lombardi

The difference between a successful person and others is not a lack of strength, not a lack of knowledge, but rather in a lack of will. ~Vincent T. Lombardi

Success is the maximum utilization of the ability that you have. ~Zig Zigler

I find that the harder I work, the more luck I seem to have. ~Thomas Jefferson

I am a great believer in luck, The harder I work, The more of it I seem to have. ~Coleman Cox

Success seems to be largely a matter of hanging on after others have let go. ~William Feather

In order to have a winner, the team must have a feeling of unity; every player must put the team first-ahead of personal glory. ~Paul Bear Bryant

Every great man is always being helped by everybody; for his gift is to get good out of all things and all persons. ~John Ruskin

It is the men behind who make the man ahead. ~Merle Crowell

If I have seen more than others, it is because I was standing on the shoulders of giants. ~Sir Isaac Newton

There is no limit to what can be accomplished if it doesn't matter who gets the credit. ~Emerson

You can accomplish much if you don't care who gets the credit. ~Ronald Reagan

Remember, nobody wins unless everybody wins. ~Bruce Springsteen

Alone we can do so little; together we can do so much. ~Helen Keller

Individual commitment to a group effort - that is what makes a team work, a company work, a society work, a civilization work. ~Vince Lombardi

There is no substitute for effort. If someone with superior natural ability permits you to outwork him, you can defeat him. If you permit someone of lesser skill to excel you in effort, he will likely excel you in accomplishment. ~Joe Robbie

If you don't make a total commitment to whatever you're doing, then you start looking to bail out the first time the boat starts leaking. It's tough enough getting that boat to shore with everybody rowing, let alone when a guy stands up and starts putting his life jacket on. ~Lou Holtz

Do you value people who won't benefit you or only those who might contribute in some way to your success? Great team players truly value others as people, and they know and relate to what others value. ~John C. Maxwell

You give 100% in the first half of the game, and if that isn't enough, in the second half you give what's left. ~Yogi Berra

The best job goes to the person who can get it done without passing the buck or coming back with excuses. ~Napoleon Hill

By the time we've made it, we've had it." ~Malcolm Forbes

Success is going from failure to failure without a loss of enthusiam. ~Sir Winston Churchill

Most people who succeed in the face of seemingly impossible conditions are people who simply don't know how to quit. ~Robert Schuller

The only place you find success before work is in the dictionary. ~Vidal Sasson

The struggle to reach the top is itself enough to fulfill the heart of man. ~Albert Camus

Success is sweet and sweeter if long delayed and gotten through many struggles and defeats. ~Amos Bronson Alcott

Obstacles are necessary for success because in selling, as in all careers of importance, victory comes only after many struggles and countless defeats. Yet, each struggle, each defeat, sharpens your skills and strengths, your courage and your endurance, your ability and your confidence and thus each obstacle is a comrade-in-arms forcing you to become better or quit. Each rebuff is an opportunity to move forward. Turn away from them, avoid them, and you throw away your future. ~Og Mandino

Coming together is a beginning, staying together is progress, and working together is success. ~Henry Ford

Let us realize that the privilege to work is a gift, that power to work is a blessing, that love of work is success. ~David O. McKay

There are no secrets to success: Don't waste time looking for them. Success is the result of perfection, hard work, learning from failure, loyalty to those for who you work,and persistence. ~General Colin Powell

A successful person is one who can lay a firm foundation with the bricks that others throw at him or her. ~David Brinkley

The secret of success is to know something nobody else knows." ~Aristotle Onassis

The secret of success is doing things not merely because they are popular, but because you deeply believe in them. ~J. Donald Walters

The secret of joy in work is contained in one word – excellence. To know how to do something well is to enjoy it. ~Pearl S. Buck

Genius is one per cent inspiration, ninety-nine per cent perspiration. ~Thomas A. Edison

Success is dependent on effort. ~Sophocles

I know the price of success: dedication, hard work, and an unremitting devotion to the things you want to see happen. ~Frank Lloyd Wright

no shortcuts to the top. They climb the mountain one step at a time. They have no use for helicopters! ~Judi Adier

The only thing that separates successful people from the ones who aren't is the willingness to work very, very hard. ~Helen Gurley Brown

I found every single successful person I've ever spoken to had a turning point. Their turning point was where they made a clear, specific, unequivocal decision that they were not going to live like this anymore. They were going to succeed. Some people make that decision at 15. Some people make it at 50. Most people never make it at all. ~Brian Tracy

Success usually comes to those who are too busy to be looking for it. ~Henry David Thoreau

If one advances confidently in the direction of his dreams, and endeavors to live the life which he has imagined, he will meet with a success unexpected in common hours. ~Henry David Thoreau

Men are born to succeed, not to fail. ~Henry David Thoreau

Recipe for Success: Study while others are sleeping; work while others are loafing; prepare while others are playing; and dream while others are wishing." ~William A. Ward

Accomplishment and success are often the result of commitment and perseverance rather than skill or talent. ~George Van Valkenburg

In this age, which believes that there is a short cut to everything, the greatest lesson to be learned is that the most difficult way is, in the long run, the easiest. ~Henry Miller

I never could have done what I have done without the habits of punctuality, order, and diligence, without the determination to concentrate myself on one subject at a time." ~Charles Dickens

'Veni, vidi, vici' (I came, I saw, I conquered). ~Julius Caesar

The man who lives for himself is a failure; the man who lives for others has achieved true success. ~Dr. Norman Vincent Peale

When you do not know what you are doing and what you are doing is the best - that is inspiration. ~Robert Bresson

Success is getting what you want. Happiness is liking what you get. ~Anonymous

Success follows doing what you want to do. There is no other way to be successful. ~Malcolm Forbes

To love what you do and feel that it matters ~ how could anything be more fun? ~Katharine Graham

Put your heart, mind, intellect and soul even to your smallest acts. This is the secret of success. ~Sivananda

Always bear in mind that your own resolution to succeed is more important than any other thing. ~Abraham Lincoln

Success is not to be pursued; it is to be attracted by the person we become. ~Jim Rohn

So celebrate what you've accomplished, but raise the bar a little higher each time you succeed. ~Mia Hamm

My mother drew a distinction between achievement and success. She said that achievement is the knowledge that you have studied and worked hard and done the best that is in you. Success is being praised by others, and that's nice, too, but not as important or satisfying. Always aim for achievement and forget about success. ~Helen Hays

The distance between insanity and genius is measured only by success. ~James Bond

Don't judge each day by the harvest you reap, but by the seeds you plant. ~Robert Louis Stevenson

Success is not the key to happiness. Happiness is the key to success. If you love what you are doing, you will be successful. ~Herman Cain

He felt about books as doctors feel about medicines, or managers about plays, cynical, but hopeful. Dame Rose Macaulay

Perhaps the most valuable result of all education is the ability to make yourself do the thing you have to do, when it ought to be done, whether you like it or not; it is the first lesson that ought to be learned; and however early a man's training begins, it is probably the last lesson that he learns thoroughly. ~Thomas H. Huxley

I must study politics and war that my sons may have liberty to study mathematics and philosophy. My sons ought to study mathematics and philosophy, geography, natural history, naval architecture, navigation, commerce, and agriculture, in order to give their children a right to study painting, poetry, music, architecture, statuary, tapestry, and porcelain. ~John Adams

Anything unattempted remains impossible. ~ Anonymous

By working faithfully eight hours a day, you may eventually get to be boss and work 12 hours a day. ~ Anonymous

Encouraged people achieve the best; dominated people achieve second best; neglected people achieve the least. . ~ Anonymous

Even a mosquito doesn't get a slap on the back until it starts to work. . ~ Anonymous

Failure is not the worst thing in the world. The very worst is not to try. ~Anonymous

Failure is the path of least persistence. ~Anonymous

Goals that are not written down are just wishes. ~Anonymous

God does not ask about our ability, but our availability. ~Anonymous

God gives us dreams a size too big so that we can grow in them. ~Anonymous

God put me on earth to accomplish a certain number of things. Right now I am so far behind I will never die! ~Anonymous

Ideas are funny little things. They don't work unless you do. ~Anonymous

If you aim at nothing, you'll hit it every time. ~Anonymous

If you don't climb the mountain, you can't view the plain. ~Anonymous

If you're not living on the edge, you're taking up too much space. ~Anonymous

In order to succeed, you must first be willing to fail. ~Anonymous

In the darkest hour the soul is replenished and given strength to continue and endure. ~Anonymous

It is wise to keep in mind that no success or failure is necessarily final. ~Anonymous

It's not the work that's hard, it's the discipline. ~Anonymous

Never be afraid to do something new. Remember, amateurs built the ark; professionals built the titanic. ~Anonymous

Only those who do nothing make no mistakes. ~Anonymous

Remember that great love and great achievements involve great risk. ~Anonymous

Self-determination is fine but needs to be tempered with self-control. ~Anonymous

Some people grin and bear it; others smile and do it. ~Anonymous

The harder you fall, the higher you bounce. ~Anonymous

The only real failure in life is the failure to try. ~Anonymous

The true gentleman does not preach his beliefs until he does so by his actions. ~Anonymous

IV. Founding Fathers

Do you want to know who you are? Don't ask. Act! Action will delineate and define you. ~Thomas Jefferson

The most valuable of all talents is that of never using two words when one will do.
~Thomas Jefferson

Honesty is the first chapter in the book of wisdom. ~Thomas Jefferson

Enlighten the people generally, and tyranny and oppressions of body and mind will vanish like evil spirits at the dawn of day. ~Thomas Jefferson

To try and fail is at least to learn. To fail to try is to suffer the loss of what might have been. ~Ben Franklin

Remember not only to say the right thing in the right place, but far more difficult still, to leave unsaid the wrong thing at the tempting moment. ~Ben Franklin

If passion drives, let reason hold the reins. ~Ben Franklin

Money never made a man happy yet, nor will it. There is nothing in its nature to produce happiness. The more a man has, the more he wants. Instead of its filling a vacuum, it makes one. ~Ben Franklin

Great beauty, great strength, and great riches are really and truly of no great use; a right heart exceeds all. ~Benjamin Franklin

Words may show a man's wit, but actions his meaning. ~Benjamin Franklin

Any fool can criticize, condemn, and complain, and most fools do. -Benjamin Franklin

Being busy does not always mean real work. The object of all work is production or accomplishment and to either of these ends there must be forethought, system, planning, intelligence, and honest purpose, as well as perspiration. Seeming to do is not doing. ~Thomas Edison

If we all did the things we are capable of doing, we would literally astound ourselves. ~Thomas A. Edison

Time is really the only capital that any human being has, and the only thing he can't afford to lose. - Thomas Edison

I find that the harder I work, the more luck I seem to have. ~Thomas Jefferson

Who dies in youth and vigor, dies the best. ~Alexander Pope

A generous heart repairs a sland'rous tongue. ~Alexander Pope

And unextinguished laughter shakes the skies. ~Alexander Pope

For fools rush in where angels fear to tread. ~Alexander Pope

Impatient straight to flesh his virgin sword. ~Alexander Pope

And love the offender, yet detest the offence. ~Alexander Pope

He serves me most who serves his country best. ~Alexander Pope

Two friends, two bodies with one soul inspired. ~Alexander Pope

In matters of style, swim with the current, In matters of principle, stand like a rock. ~Thomas Jefferson

We built this country on certain principle, see ye to it; remain faithful. ~Founding Fathers

Content makes poor men rich; discontent makes rich men poor. ~Benjamin Franklin

When one door closes another door opens: but we often look so long and so regretfully upon the closed door. ~Alexander Graham Bell

How long a minute is, depends on which side of the bathroom door you're on. ~Zall's Second Law

I expect to pass through this life but once. If, therefore there can be any kindness I can show or any good thing I can do for any fellow being let me do it now...as I shall not pass this way again. ~William Penn

Those who stand for nothing fall for anything. ~Alexander Hamilton

I have not failed. I've just found 10,000 ways that won't work. ~Thomas A. Edison

V. Funny Quotes

It is important to learn to laugh, and maybe more important, learning to laugh at oneself -- when it is necessary. Laughter can lighten most, if not all, tense situations. Think of someone you know that doesn't laugh or smile very often. How do you feel in their presence? Is it awkward? Is it hard to be around them? No one wants to be around a grump because it can be contagious. Influencing those around the grump to feel uncomfortable, and where one is uncomfortable it is hard to have good feelings. So, "Laugh like no one is watching..."

Two things are infinite: the universe and human stupidity; and I'm not sure about the universe. ~Albert Einstein

Insanity: Doing the same thing over and over again and expecting different results. ~Albert Einstein

"When you are courting a nice girl an hour seems like a second. When you sit on a red-hot cinder a second seems like an hour. That's relativity. ~Albert Einstein

If a cluttered desk is that of a cluttered mind, of what, then, is an empty desk? ~Albert Einstein

If you are going through hell, keep going. ~Winston S. Churchill

I like work: it fascinates me. I can sit and look at it for hours. ~Jerome K. Jerome

Life moves pretty fast. If you don't stop to look around once in a while you could miss it. ~From the movie Ferris Bueller's Day Off

I can't sit still and see another man slaving and working. I want to get up and superintend, and walk round with my hands in my pockets, and tell him what to do. It is my energetic nature. I can't help it. ~Jerome K. Jerome

Being a woman is a terribly difficult task, since it consists principally in dealing with men. ~Joseph Conrad

Keep your eyes wide open before marriage, half shut afterwards. ~Benjamin Franklin

I wake up every morning at nine and grab for the morning paper. Then I look at the obituary page. If my name is not on it, I get up. ~Benjamin Franklin

Those who think they have not time for bodily exercise will sooner or later have to find time for illness. ~Edward Stanley

You complain that you don't have the time to exercise, and that's fine. But just do one sit-up. While you're down there, do 29 more.— Unknown

I can only please one person per day, today is not your day and tomorrow doesn't look good either. ~Unknown

You know you're in love when you can't fall asleep because reality is finally better than your dreams. ~Dr. Seuss

The fact that we live at the bottom of a deep gravity well, on the surface of a gas covered planet going around a nuclear fireball 90 million miles away and think this to be normal is obviously some indication of how skewed our perspective tends to be. ~Douglas Adams

If anyone spends almost the whole day in reading...he gradually loses the capacity for thinking...This is the case with many learned persons; they have read themselves stupid
~Arthur Schopenhauer

Always remember you're unique, just like everyone else.

Nobody can be exactly like me. Sometimes even I have trouble doing it. ~Tallulah Bankhead

As we grow as unique persons, we learn to respect the uniqueness of others. ~Rober Schuller

Adults are obsolete children. ~Dr. Seuss

Whether you're a man or a woman the fascination resides in finding out that we're alike. ~Marguerite Duras

The only certainty is that nothing is certain. ~Pliny the Elder

I never wanted to be famous. I only wanted to be great. ~Ray Charles

There is only one thing in the world worse than being talked about, and that is not being talked about. ~Oscar Wilde

How did it get so late so soon?
It's night before it's afternoon.
December is here before it's June.
My goodness how the time has flewn.
How did it get so late so soon?
~Dr. Seuss

Nobody goes there anymore, it's too crowded. ~Yogi Berra

We cannot really love anybody with whom we never laugh. ~Agnes Repplier

He deserves Paradise who makes his companions laugh. ~Anonymous

The more you find out about the world, the more opportunities there are to laugh at it. ~Bill Nye,

Laughter gives us distance. It allows us to step back from an event, deal with it and then move on. ~Bob Newhart

Total absence of humor renders life impossible. ~Colette

Laughter is by definition healthy. ~Doris Lessing

The most wasted of all days is one without laughter. ~E. E. Cummings

If you don't learn to laugh at trouble, you won't have anything to laugh at when you're old. ~Edgar Watson Howe

Laugh at yourself first, before anyone else can. ~Elsa Maxwell,

You cannot be mad at somebody who makes you laugh - it's as simple as that. ~Jay Leno

If we couldn't laugh, we would all go insane. ~Jimmy Buffett

In this life he laughs longest who laughs last. ~John Masefield

Man is distinguished from all other creatures by the faculty of laughter. ~Joseph Addison

One doesn't have a sense of humor. It has you. ~Larry Gelbart

Always laugh when you can. It is cheap medicine. ~Lord Byron

The human race has one really effective weapon, and that is laughter. ~Mark Twain

You don't stop laughing because you grow old. You grow old because you stop laughing. ~Michael Pritchard

Laughter is inner jogging. ~Norman Cousins

I was irrevocably betrothed to laughter, the sound of which has always seemed to me to be the most civilized music in the world. ~Peter Ustinov

You can't deny laughter; when it comes, it plops down in your favorite chair and stays as long as it wants. ~Stephen King

Beware of too much laughter, for it deadens the mind and produces oblivion. ~The Talmud

Laughter is the closest distance between two people. ~Victor Borge

Among those whom I like or admire, I can find no common denominator, but among those whom I love, I can: all of them make me laugh. ~W. H. Auden

If you stand up and be counted, from time to time you may get yourself knocked down. But remember this: A man flattened by an opponent can get up again. A man flattened by conformity stays down for good. ~Thomas J. Watson

Normal is not something you aspire to, it's something to get away from. ~Jodie Foster

The closest to perfection a person ever comes is when he fills out a job application form. ~Evan Esar

Bad habits are like a comfortable bed, easy to get into, but hard to get out of. ~Unknown

Credibility, like virginity, can only be lost once and never recovered. ~Charley Reese

Being a husband is a whole-time job. ~Arnold Bennett

This is like deja vu all over again. ~Yogi Berra

Never put off until tomorrow what you can do the day after tomorrow. ~ Mark Twain

Hard work often pays off after time, but laziness always pays off now. ~Larry Kersten

Trying is the first step towards failure. ~Homer Simpson

One of the greatest labour-saving inventions of today is tomorrow. ~ Vincent T Foss

Every generation imagines itself to be more intelligent than the one that went before it, and wiser than the one that comes after it. ~George Orwell

He who demands little gets it. ~Ellen Glasgow

A thing worth having is a thing worth cheating for. ~W.C. Fields

He who dies with the most toys is, nonetheless, still dead. ~Unknown

The learned man knows that he is ignorant. ~Victor Hugo

He who laughs last, thinks slowest. ~Confucius

In this life he laughs longest who laughs last. ~John Masefield

It's noble to be good. It's nobler to teach others to be good, and less trouble. ~Mark Twain

Do not do unto others as you would that they should do unto you. Their tastes may not be the same. ~George Bernard Shaw

Spoon feeding in the long run teaches us nothing but the shape of the spoon. ~E.M. Forster

People will pay more to be entertained than educated. ~Johnny [John William] Carson

Sometimes it is harder to deprive oneself of a pain than of a pleasure. ~F. Scott Fitzgerald

Quotations can be valuable, like raisins in the rice pudding, for adding iron as well as eye appeal. ~Peg Bracken

We know what happens to people who stay in the middle of the road. They get run over. ~Aneurin Bevan

The only things in the middle of the road are yellow stripes and dead armadillos. ~Jim Hightower

Standing in the middle of the road is very dangerous; you get knocked down by the traffic from both sides. ~Margaret Thatcher

Middle age is when your age starts to show around your middle. ~Bob Hope

If I were two-faced, would I be wearing this one? ~Abraham Lincoln

It is the dull man who is always sure, and the sure man who is always dull. ~H.L. Mencken

I apologize for the long letter but I didn't have the time to write a short one. ~Thomas Jefferson

Essays should be like miniskirts. Short enough to be attractive, yet long enough to cover the main parts. ~Unknown

Do not bite at the bait of pleasure till you know there is no hook beneath it. ~Thomas Jefferson

If you want to succeed in life...you must pick 3 bones to carry with you at all times: a wish bone, a backbone, and a funny bone. ~Reba McEntire

If at first you don't succeed, try, try again. Then quit. No use being a damn fool about it. ~W.C. Fields

About the time we think we can make ends meet, somebody moves the ends. ~Herbert Hoover

There comes a time in every man's life and I've had many of them. ~Casey Stengel

Talk sense to a fool and he calls you foolish. ~Euripides

The root of not listening is knowing. If I already know the truth, why do I need to listen to you? ~Adam Kahane

I haven't failed, I've found ten thousand ways that don't work. ~Ben Franklin

I have not failed. I've just found 10,000 ways that won't work. ~Thomas Alva Edison

Have you ever noticed? Anybody going slower than you is an idiot, and anyone going faster than you is a moron. ~George Carlin

All the people like us are We, and everyone else is They. ~Rudyard Kipling

Remember if people talk behind your back, it only means you are two steps ahead. ~Fannie Flagg

Everything is funny as long as it is happening to somebody else. ~Will Rogers

Some cause happiness wherever they go; others whenever they go. ~Oscar Wilde

People seem to enjoy things more when they know a lot of other people have been left out of the pleasure. ~Russel Baker

If it's sanity you're after, there's no recipe like laughter. ~Henry Rutherford Elliot

I always turn to the sports pages first, which records people's accomplishments. The front page has nothing but man's failures. ~Chief Justice Earl Warren

If I had my life to live again, I'd make the same mistakes, only sooner. ~Tallulah Bankhead

Worry is interest paid on trouble before it is due. ~William Inge

Statistics are like bikinis. What they reveal is suggestive, but what they conceal is vital. ~Aaron Levenstein

Between two products equal in price, function and quality, the better looking will outsell the other. ~Raymond Loewy

Beauty is in the eye of the beholder, and it may be necessary from time to time to give a stupid or misinformed beholder a black eye. ~Miss Piggy

Good communication is as stimulating as black coffee and just as hard to sleep after. ~Anne Morrow Lindbergh

Don't knock the weather; nine-tenths of the people couldn't start a conversation if it didn't change once in a while. ~Kin Hubbard

I no longer worry about being a brilliant conversationalist. I simply try to be a good listener. I notice that people who do that are usually welcome wherever they go. ~Frank Bettger

An education is like a crumbling building that needs constant upkeep with repairs and additions. ~Edith Wharton

Ask a question and you're a fool for three minutes; do not ask a question and you're a fool for the rest of your life. ~Chinese Proverb

There are no foolish questions, and no man becomes a fool until he has stopped asking questions. ~Charles Proteus Steinmetz

Don't be afraid to ask dumb questions. They're more easily handled than dumb mistakes. ~William Wister Hanes

There is nobody so irritating as somebody with less intelligence and more sense than we have. ~Don Herold

A pessimist is someone who complains about the noise when opportunity knocks. ~Michael Levine

Opportunity may knock only once, but temptation leans on the doorbell. ~Anonymous

If you are going through hell, keep going. ~Sir Winston Churchill

A lie told often enough becomes truth. ~Lenin

Life is the garment we continually alter, but which never seems to fit. ~David McCord

If you want to make enemies, try to change something. ~Woodrow Wilson

Forgive your enemies, but never forget their names. ~John F. Kennedy

Friends may come and go, but enemies accumulate. ~Thomas Jones

When you are down and out, something always turns up - usually the noses of your friends. ~Orson Welles

Acquaintance: A person whom we know well enough to borrow from, but not well enough to lend to. ~Ambrose Bierce

If you'd know the value of money, go and borrow some. ~Benjamin Franklin

A bank is a place that will lend you money if you can prove that you don't need it. ~Bob Hope

Money frees you from doing things you dislike. Since I dislike doing nearly everything, money is handy. ~Groucho Marx

A man cannot be too careful in the choice of his enemies. ~Oscar Wilde

Be kind to everyone you talk with. You never know who's going to be on the jury. ~Tiger Goldstick

I argue very well. Ask any of my remaining friends. I can win an argument on any topic, against any opponent. People know this, and steer clear of me at parties. Often, as a sign of their great respect, they don't even invite me. ~Dave Barry

Love thy neighbor as yourself, but choose your neighborhood. ~Louise Beal

Some people like my advice so much that they frame it upon the wall instead of using it. ~Gordon R. Dickson

A free society is a place where it's safe to be unpopular. ~Adlai Stevenson

I love Mickey Mouse more than any woman I have ever known. ~Walt Disney

A celebrity is a person who works hard all his life to become known, then wears dark glasses to avoid being recognized. ~Fred Allen

He has the gift of quiet. ~John Le Carre

When you have nothing to say, say nothing. ~Charles Caleb Colton

People have to talk about something just to keep their good voice boxes in working order, so they'll have good voice boxes in case there's ever anything really meaningful to say. ~Kurt Vonnegut Jr.

Nothing is swifter than rumor. ~Horace

Put your hand on a hot stove for a minute, and it seems like an hour. Sit with a pretty girl for an hour, and it seems like a minute. THAT'S relativity. ~Albert Einstein

If love is the answer, could you rephrase the question? ~Lily Tomlin

The trouble with women is that they get all excited about nothing and then they marry him. ~Cher

Two wrongs don't make a right, but they make a good excuse. ~Thomas Szasz

To keep your marriage brimming, with love in the loving cup, whenever you're wrong, admit it; whenever you're right, shut up. ~Ogden Nash

Many people would sooner die than think; In fact, they do so. ~Bertrand Russell

The brain can be developed just the same as the muscles can be developed, if one will only take the pains to train the mind to think. Why do so many men never amount to anything? Because they don't think. ~Thomas Edison

The mind is not a vessel to be filled but a fire to be kindled. ~Plutarch

If love means never having to say you're sorry, then marriage means always having to say everything twice. ~Estelle Getty

Keep thy eyes wide open before marriage and half shut afterwards. ~Benjamin Franklin

The only true love is love at first sight; second sight dispels it. ~Israel Zangwill

What is important is that one is capable of love. It is perhaps the only glimpse we are permitted of eternity. ~Helen Hayes

Those who love deeply never grow old; they may die of old age, but they die young. ~Sir Arthur Wing Pinero

No matter how happily a woman may be married, it always pleases her to discover that there is a nice man who wishes that she were not. ~H. L. Mencken

Look after your wife; never mind yourself , she'll look after you. ~Sacha Guitry

Some of us are becoming the men we wanted to marry. ~Gloria Steinem

Behind every successful man is a woman, behind her is his wife. ~Groucho Marx

Success is often the result of taking a misstep in the right direction. ~Al Bernstein

As the purse is emptied, the heart is filled. ~Victor Hugo

A woman who thinks she is intelligent demands the same rights as man. An intelligent woman gives up. ~Sidnonie Gabrielle Colette

Many a man owes his success to his first wife and his second wife to his success. ~Jim Backus

The old believe everything, the middle-aged suspect everything, the young know everything. ~Oscar Wilde

We spend the first twelve months of our children's lives teaching them to walk and talk and the next twelve telling them to sit down and shut up. ~Phyllis Diller

In raising my children, I have lost my mind but found my soul. ~Lisa T. Shepherd

I never forget a face, but in your case I'll make an exception. ~Groucho

Some of the world's greatest feats were accomplished by people not smart enough to know they were impossible. ~Doug Larson

The leadership instinct you are born with is the backbone. You develop the funny bone and the wishbone that go with it. ~Elaine Agather

Success is not the result of spontaneous combustion. You must set yourself on fire. ~Reggie Leach

Opportunities are usually disguised as hard work, so most people don't recognize them. ~Ann Landers

Opportunity may knock only once, but temptation leans on the doorbell. ~Anonymous

Here is the test to find whether your mission on earth is finished: If you're alive, it isn't. ~Richard Bach

The secret of success is sincerity. Once you can fake that, you've got it made. ~Jean Giraudoux

I was asked to memorise what I did not understand; and, my memory being so good, it refused to be insulted in that manner. ~Aleister Crowley

Make yourself an honest man and then you may be sure there is one less rascal in the world. ~Thomas Carlyle

The fool doth think he is wise, while the wise man knows himself a fool. ~William Shakespeare

Imagination was given to man to compensate him for what he is not; a sense of humor to console him for what he is. ~Francis Bacon

To read without reflecting is like eating without digesting. ~Edmund Burke

All a man can betray is his conscience. ~Joseph Conrad

I think the surest sign that there is intelligent life out there in the universe is that none of it has tried to contact us. ~Calvin & Hobbes

Don't take life seriously because you can't come out of it alive. ~Warren Miller

Some people who yearn for endless life don't even know what to do with a rainy afternoon. ~Harvey H. Potthoff

People don't ask for facts in making up their minds. They would rather have one good, soul-satisfying emotion than a dozen facts. ~Robert Keith Leavit

Be very, very careful what you put into that head, because you will never, ever get it out. ~Thomas Cardinal Wolsey

There's a mighty big difference between good, sound reasons and reasons that sound good. ~Burton Hills

We have 40 million reasons for failure, but not a single excuse. ~Rudyard Kipling

99% of the failures come from people who have the habit of making excuses. ~George Washington Carver

Everybody lies, but it doesn't matter because nobody listens. ~Nick Diamos

People demand freedom of speech to make up for the freedom of thought which they avoid ~Soren Aabye Kierkegaard

When you choose the lesser of two evils, always remember that it is still an evil. ~Max Lerner

When choosing between two evils, I always like to try the one I've never tried before. ~Mae West

You must learn from the mistakes of others. You can't possibly live long enough to make them all yourself. ~Sam Levenson

There is never enough time, unless you are serving it. ~Malcolm Forbes

The brain can be seen as a complex machine, like a gooey computer. ~Robert C. Solomon

Television: A medium. So called because it is neither rare nor well done. ~Ernie Kovacs

One of the first duties of the physician is to educate the masses not to take medicine. ~Sir William Osler

Don't throw away the old bucket until you know whether the new one holds water. ~Swedish proverb

Of all the things I've lost I miss my mind the most. ~ Unknown

Minds are like parachutes, they function only when open. ~ Unknown

Those who can laugh without cause have either found the true meaning of happiness or have gone stark raving mad. ~Norm Papernick

Happiness is no laughing matter. ~Richard Whately

Happiness is nothing more than good health and a bad memory. ~Albert Schweitzer

Happiness is good health and a bad memory. ~Ingrid Bergman

Life is something to do when you can't get to sleep. ~Fran Lebowitz

I have noticed that the people who are late are often so much jollier than the people who have to wait for them. ~E.V. Lucas

Punctuality is the politeness of kings. ~King Louis XVIII

You can't be truly rude until you understand good manners. ~Rita Mae Brown

Good manners will open doors that the best education cannot. ~Clarence Thomas

There is no pleasure in having nothing to do. The fun is in having lots to do and not doing it. ~Mary Wilson Little

The greatest inspiration is often born of desperation. ~Comer Cotrell

The longing to produce great inspirations didn't produce anything but more longing. ~Sophie Kerr

The time you enjoy wasting is not wasting time. ~T.S. Elliot

England and America are two countries separated by the same language. ~George Bernard Shaw

VI. Freedom

No man is above the law and no man is below it; nor do we ask any man's permission when we ask him to obey it. ~Theodore Roosevelt

Liberty is always dangerous, but it is the safest thing we have. ~Harry Emerson Fosdick

A patriot must always be ready to defend his country against his government. ~Edward Abbey

Government is not the problem, and government is not the solution. We, the American people, we are the solution. ~President Clinton

I would rather be exposed to the inconveniences attending too much liberty than those attending too small a degree of it. ~Thomas Jefferson

Obedience to the law is demanded as a right; not asked as a favor. ~Theodore Roosevelt

To announce that there must be no criticism of the President, or that we are to stand by the President, right or wrong, is not only unpatriotic and servile, but is morally treasonable to the American public. ~Theodore Roosevelt

The things that will destroy America are prosperity at any price, peace at any price, safety first instead of duty first, and love of soft living and the get-rich-quick theory of life. ~Theodore Roosevelt

Peace is not merely a distant goal that we seek, but a means by which we arrive at that goal. ~Martin Luther King Jr.

We look forward to the time when the power to love will replace the love of power. Then will our world know the blessings of peace. ~William Edwart Gladstone

No government can be long secure without a formidable opposition. ~Benjamin Disraeli

Politics is war without bloodshed while war is politics with bloodshed. ~Mao Tse-tung

Politics, very often, is simply economics pursued by other means. ~Edward J. Nell

You can tell the ideals of a nation by its advertising. ~Norman Douglas

A government which takes from Peter to pay Paul will always have the support of Paul. ~George Bernard Shaw

So you think that money is the root of all evil. Have you ever asked what is the root of all money? ~Ayn Rand

You're not supposed to be so blind with patriotism that you can't face reality. Wrong is wrong, no matter who says it. ~Malcolm X

I was born an American; I will live an American; I shall die an American. ~Daniel Webster

Let every nation know, whether it wishes us well or ill, that we shall pay any price, bear any burden, meet any hardship, support any friend, oppose any foe to assure the survival and success of freedom. ~John F. Kennedy

We will not waver; we will not tire; we will not falter; and we will not fail. Peace and freedom will prevail. ~ George W. Bush

In the truest sense freedom cannot be bestowed, it must be achieved. ~Franklin D. Roosevelt

Freedom is hammered out on the anvil of discussion, dissent, and debate. ~Hubert H. Humphrey

Freedom is not worth having if it does not include the freedom to make mistakes. ~Gandhi

Our lives begin to end the day we become silent about things that matter. ~Martin Luther King, Jr.

We must learn to live together as brothers or perish together as fools. ~Martin Luther King Jr.

Let JUSTICE be done though the heavens fall. ~Roman maxim

Injustice anywhere is a threat to justice everywhere. ~Rev. Martin Luther King, Jr.

True peace is not merely the absence of tension: it is the presence of justice. ~Martin Luther King Jr.

I have always found that mercy bears richer fruits than strict justice. ~Abraham Lincoln

The true charter of liberty is independence, maintained by force. ~Voltaire

You can't separate peace from freedom because no one can be at peace unless he has his freedom. ~Malcolm X

The day that the black man takes an uncompromising step and realizes that he's within his rights, when his own freedom is being jeopardized, to use any means necessary to bring about his freedom or put a halt to that injustice, I don't think he'll be by himself. ~Malcolm X

We declare our right on this earth...to be a human being, to be respected as a human being, to be given the rights of a human being in this society, on this earth, in this day, which we intend to bring into existence by any means necessary. ~Malcolm X

We are going to have peace even if we have to fight for it. ~Dwight D. Eisenhower

Freedom is rarely lost in a single stroke. The danger lies in losing it bit by bit. ~Dennis Patrick

All censorships exist to prevent any one from challenging current conceptions and existing institutions. All progress is initiated by challenging current conceptions, and executed by supplanting existing institutions. Consequently the first condition of progress is the removal of censorships. ~George Bernard Shaw

I disapprove of what you say, but I will defend to the death your right to say it. ~Voltaire

Liberty will not descend to a people; a people must raise themselves to liberty; it is a blessing that must be earned before it can be enjoyed. ~Charles Colton

VII. Goals

Goal setting is essential in order to see and measure improvement. Without goals one is just strolling down a street with many side roads. One can end up miles on a false road before it is realized. One can go months or years just driving along not really having any idea where one is headed. Goals give one direction and purpose. To achieve a goal one must know what is sought -- something specific. One's desire to reach a goal must be greater than the pain one experiences in reaching it.

In order to feel happiness it is paramount that we feel fulfillment. Goals help us reach this end. A sense of pride from accomplishment, a sense of achievement from reaching a goal helps us build self-confidence.

It doesn't matter which road we take if we don't have a desination. The more goals we set the more on the path we will feel, the more fulfillment we will feel, the more joy we will be experiencing.

I have not failed 10,000 times. I have successfully found 10,000 ways that will not work. ~Thomas Edison

When one door closes another door opens: but we often look so long and so regretfully upon the closed door.~Alexander Graham Bell

Live your life each day as you would climb a mountain. An occasional glance toward the summit keeps the goal in mind, but many beautiful scenes are to be observed from each new vantage point. Climb slowly, steadily, enjoying each passing moment; and the view from the summit will serve as a fitting climax for the journey- - Harold B. Melchart

The only one who can tell you that you can't is you, but you don't have to listen! ~Vince Lombardi

Nobody, on their deathbed, ever said, “I wish I'd spent more time at the office. ~Stephen Covey

Imagination is not a talent of some men but is the health of every man. ~Ralph Waldo Emerson

If you don't start, it's certain you won't arrive. ~Unknown

If you don't know where you are going, any road will get you there. ~Lewis Carroll

A goal is created three times. First as a mental picture. Second, when written down to add clarity and dimension. And third, when you take action towards its achievement. ~Gary Ryan Blair

Are you bored with life? Then throw yourself into some work you believe in with all your heart, live for it, die for it, and you will find happiness that you had thought could never be yours. ~Dale Carnegie

He who chooses the beginning of the road chooses the place it leads to. It is the means that determines the end. ~Harry Emerson Fosdick

Dream as if you'll live forever. Live as if you'll die today. ~James Dean

The roads we take are more important than the goals we announce. Decisions determine destiny. ~Frederick Speakman

If you don't know where you are going, you will probably end up somewhere else. ~Laurence J. Peter

The ultimate reason for setting goals is to entice you to become the person it takes to achieve them. ~Jim Rohn

Goals are your personal statements of what you are truly willing to do to achieve what you really want to achieve. ~Denis Waitley

Setting goals for your game is an art. The trick is in setting them at the right level neither too low nor too high. ~Greg Norman

You are never really playing against an opponent. You are playing against yourself, your own highest standards. And when you reach your limits, that is real joy. ~Arthur Ashe

Don't set your goals too low. If you don't need much, you won't become much. ~Jim Rohn

Setting goals provides man with an excuse to stop before he has exhausted all efforts to reach his maximum potential. ~David V. Ellison

A dream is your creative vision for your life in the future. A goal is what specifically you intend to make happen. Dreams and goals should be just out of your present reach but not out of sight. Dreams and goals are coming attractions in your life. ~Joseph Campbell

Reach high, for the stars lie hidden in your soul. Dream deep, for every dream precedes the goal. ~Pamela Vaull Starr

Before your dreams can come true, you have to have those dreams. ~Joyce Brothers

Cherish your visions and your dreams as they are the children of your soul; the blue prints of your ultimate achievements. ~Napoleon Hill

No one rises to low expectations. ~Jesse Jackson

Aim at perfection in everything, though in most things it is unattainable. However, they who aim at it, and persevere, will come much nearer to it than those whose laziness and despondency make them give it up as unattainable. ~Lord Chesterfield

Perfection is achieved, not when there is nothing more to add, but when there is nothing left to take away. ~Antoine de Saint Exupery

Every life form seems to strive to its maximum except human beings. How tall will a tree grow? As tall as it possibly can. Human beings, on the other hand, have been given the dignity of choice. You can choose to be all or you can choose to be less. Why not stretch up to the full measure of the challenge and see what all you can do? ~Jim Rohn

To accomplish great things, we must not only act, but also dream; not only plan, but also believe. ~Anatole France

I learned that there were two ways I could live my life: following my dreams or doing something else. Dreams aren't a matter of chance, but a matter of choice. When I dream, I believe I am rehearsing my future. ~David Copperfield

The passionate ones, the ones who go after what they want, may not get what they want, but they remain vital, in touch with themselves, and when they lie on their deathbeds, they have few regrets. ~Charlie Kaufman

We are what we repeatedly do. Excellence then is not an act but a habit. ~Aristotle

Excellence can be attained if you Care more than others think is wise, Risk more than others think is safe, Dream more than others think is practical, and Expect more than others think is possible. ~ Unknown

When you have a dream you've got to grab it and never let go. ~Carol Burnett

All our dreams can come true, if we have the courage to pursue them. ~Walt Disney

It may be that those who do most, dream most. ~Stephen Leacock

Dreams do not vanish, so long as people do not abandon them. ~Phantom F. Harlock

Hold fast to dreams, for if dreams die, life is a broken bird that cannot fly. ~Langston Hughes

To aim at excellence, our reputation, and friends, and all must be ventured; to aim at the average we run no risk and provide little service. ~Oliver Goldsmith

Your vision will become clear only when you look into your heart. Who looks outside, dreams. Who looks inside, awakens. ~Carl Gustav Jung

The free man is he who does not fear to go to the end of his thought. ~Leon Blum

Great souls have wills; feeble ones only have wishes. ~Chinese Proverb

Excellence is the gradual result of always striving to do better. ~Pat Riley

The tragedy of life doesn't lie in not reaching your goal. The tragedy lies in having no goal to reach. ~Benjamin Mays

People who are unable to motivate themselves must be content with mediocrity, no matter how impressive their other talents. ~Andrew Carnegie

Many are stubborn in pursuit of the path they have chosen, few in pursuit of the goal. ~Friedrich Nietzsche

The real tragedy of life is not in being limited to one talent, but in the failure to use that one talent. ~Edgar W. Work

Go confidently in the direction of your dreams! Live the life you've imagined. As you simplify your life, the laws of the universe will be simpler. ~Henry David Thoreau

A scholar who cherishes the love of comfort is not fit to be deemed a scholar. ~Lao-Tzu

Goals... There's no telling what you can do when you get inspired by them. There's no telling what you can do when you believe in them.

There's no telling what will happen when you act upon them. ~Jim Rohn

If one does not know to which port one is sailing, no wind is favorable. ~Seneca

The richness of the human experience would lose something of rewarding joy if there were no limitations to overcome. ~Helen Keller

Always aim for achievement, and forget about success. ~Helen Hayes

The big challenge is to become all that you have the possibility of becoming. You cannot believe what it does to the human spirit to maximize your human potential and stretch yourself to the limit. ~Jim Rohn

I have found that being honest is the best technique I can use. Right up front, tell people what you're trying to accomplish and what you're willing to sacrifice to accomplish it ~Lee Iacocca

The true worth of a man is to be measured by the objects he pursues. ~Marcus Aureleus

What's more important-your goal, or others' opinions of your goal. ~unknown

People who say life is not worthwhile are really saying that they themselves have no personal goals which are worthwhile. Get yourself a goal worth working for. Better still, get yourself a project. Always have something ahead of you to "look forward to" --to work for and to hope for. ~Maxwell Maltz

VIII. Great Reformers

Cowardice asks the question, "Is it safe?" Expediency asks the question, "Is it politic?" Vanity asks the question, "Is it popular?" But, conscience asks the question, "Is it right?" And there comes a time when one must take a position that is neither safe, nor politic, nor popular, but one must take it because one's conscience tells one that it is right. ~Dr. Martin Luther King, Jr.

The time is always right to do what is right. ~Dr. Martin Luther King, Jr.

Truth resides in every human heart, and one has to search for it there, and to be guided by truth as one sees it. But no one has a right to coerce others to act according to his own view of truth. ~Mahatma Mohandas K. Gandhi

In matters of conscience, the law of the majority has no place. ~Gandhi

Happiness is when what you think, what you say, and what you do are in harmony.
~Mahatma Gandhi

You must be the change you wish to see in the world. ~Mahatma Gandhi

There would be no one to frighten you if you refused to be afraid. ~Mohandas K. Gandhi

The weak can never forgive. Forgiveness is the attribute of the strong. ~Mahatma Gandhi

To lose patience is to lose the battle. ~Mahatma Gandhi

I should love to satisfy all, if I possibly can; but in trying to satisfy all, I may be able to satisfy none. I have, therefore, arrived at the conclusion that the best course is to satisfy one's own conscience and leave the world to form its own judgment, favorable or otherwise. ~Mohandas K. Gandhi

IX. Life

Life is full of challenges. Let it not be forgotten it is through our challenges and tribulations that we build character. We become the person we are through adversity. Without experiences we would never become anyone of great worth. We would never experience love or happiness if we never experienced hate and sadness. We experience both phenomena that we may choose, with a more sure knowledge, which we would rather have.

It is no secret that people are able to feel happiness and joy amidst tragedy of war torn nations. The secret is how they attain this state even when things look so bleak. Surly it is easy to see past this masquerade the world paints, "the more the better." The world portrays a dangerous misconception that many people fall trap to. Money, power, full filling our every whim is the way to happiness. The attitude of "more is better", "give me", and "I deserve more." This misconception seldom brings the satisfaction we desire. It might be said this idea of bringing the greatest sense of happiness, in fact, seems to bring the least. It seems every human soul is ingrained with basic needs; needs that are seldom in this way fulfilled. It's amazing how the western world measures contentment, happiness, or joy as having abundance. Yet, when studies are done it would seem those countries that would fall under poverty stricken nations are on the whole, happier then the western world. Maybe it's true, "richness is not measured by the things one has, but by the things one doesn't need,"

Life is full of choices, and many choices we are forced to make from outside forces; nonetheless, the choice is always how we will react personally to a circumstance we might find ourselves.

The tragedy of life is not that it ends so soon, but that we wait so long to begin it. ~Richard Evens

No dream comes true until you wake up and go to work. ~ Ralph Engelstad

The harder I work, the luckier I get. ~ Mark Twain

Determine never to be idle. No person will have occasion to complain of the want of time, who never loses any. It is wonderful how much may be done, if we are always doing.
~Thomas Jefferson

To each there comes in their lifetime a special moment when they are figuratively tapped on the shoulder and offered the chance to do a very special thing, unique to them and fitted to their talents. What a tragedy if that moment finds them unprepared or unqualified for that which could have been their finest hour. ~Winston S. Churchill

Life is like riding a bicycle. To keep your balance, you must keep moving. ~Albert Einstein

Our lives begin to end the day we become silent about things that matter. ~Martin Luther King Jr.

Compared with what we ought to be, we are only half awake. ~ William James

Being humble means recognizing that we are not on earth to see how important we can become, but to see how much difference we can make in the lives of others.~ Gordon B. Hinckley

Do the best you can. But I want to emphasize that it be the very best. We are too prone to be satisfied with mediocre performance. We are capable of doing so much better. ~Gordon B. Hinckley

The cause of most of man's unhappiness is sacrificing what he wants most for what he wants now. ~Gordon B. Hinckley

The key to happiness is having dreams. The key to success is making your dreams come true. ~Anonymous

Life is not measured by the number of breaths we take, but by the moments that take our breath away. ~ Unknown

Life is 10% what happens to you and 90% what you do with what happens to you! Anonymous

Pain is inevitable. Suffering is optional. ~M. Kathleen Casey

Do not go where the path may lead, go instead where there is no path and leave a trail. ~ Ralph Waldo Emerson

The man who follows the crowd will usually get no further than the crowd. The man who walks alone is likely to find himself in places no one has ever been. ~Alan Ashley-Pitt

You can discover more about a person in an hour of play than in a year of conversation. ~Plato

You will never know until you do it. Surprise yourself; do the unexpected. Go outside your comfort zone.

It is not the critic who counts; not the man who points out how the strong man stumbles, or where the doer of deeds could have done them better. The credit belongs to the man who is actually in the arena, whose face is marred by dust and sweat and blood; who strives valiantly; who errs, who comes short again and again, because there is no effort without error and shortcoming; but who does actually strive to do the deeds; who knows great enthusiasms, the great devotions; who spends himself in a worthy cause; who at the best knows in the end the triumph of high achievement, and who at the worst, if he fails, at least fails while daring greatly, so that his place shall never be with those cold and timid souls who neither know victory nor defeat. ~Theodore Roosevelt

There are no mistakes. The events we bring upon ourselves, no matter how unpleasant, are necessary in order to learn what we need to learn; whatever steps we take, they're necessary to reach the places we've chosen to go. ~Richard Bach

If you want to keep your memories, you first have to live them. ~Bob Dylan

Failure is just another way to learn how to do something right. ~Marian Wright Edelman

Experience is not what happens to a man; it is what a man does with what happens to him. ~Aldous Huxley

Experience is a hard teacher because she gives the test first, the lesson afterwards. ~Vernon Sanders Law

Experience is simply the name we give our mistakes. ~Oscar Wilde

Good judgment is usually the result of experience. And experience is frequently the result of bad judgment. But to learn from the experience of others requires those who have the experience to share the knowledge with those who follow. ~Barry LePatner

Experience is the name everyone gives to his mistakes. ~Elbert Hubbard

Life is a succession of lessons which must be lived to be understood. ~Helen Keller

You will not grow if you sit in a beautiful flower garden, but you will grow if you are sick, if you are in pain, if you experience losses, and if you do not put your head in the sand, but take the pain and learn to accept it, not as a curse or punishment but as a gift to you with a very, very specific purpose. ~Elizabeth Kubler-Ross

The reward of suffering is experience. ~Aeschylus

It's fine to celebrate success, but it is more important to heed the lessons of failure. ~Bill Gates

There is only one thing more painful than learning from experience and that is not learning from experience. ~Archibald McLeish

Good judgement comes from experience, and often experience comes from bad judgement. ~Rita Mae Brown

He who learns but does not think, is lost! He who thinks but does not learn is in great danger. ~Confucius

Experience is a wonderful thing; it enables you to recognize a mistake every time you make it. ~The Associated Press

There are some things you learn best in calm, and some in storm. ~Willa Cather

There is nothing so easy to learn as experience and nothing so hard to apply. ~Josh Billings

Age is only a number, a cipher for the records. A man can't retire his experience. He must use it. Experience achieves more with less energy and time. ~Bernard Mannes Baruch

I never let schooling interfere with my education. ~Mark Twain

Education is what you get from reading the fine print. Experience is what you get from not reading it. ~Uknown

Education is what survives when what has been learnt has been forgotten. ~B. F. Skinner

Experience is what you get when you don't get what you want. ~Dan Stanford

Success is a lousy teacher. It seduces smart people into thinking they can't lose. ~Bill Gates

X. Love

Love is one of the strongest emotions we can experience. It can drive us to do extreme things—in the name of love. Its opposite can be just as strong. The difference is one is constructive while the other is destructive. It is through love that war sees a dramatic change; hate never brings good results. Sooner or later hate will come back to bite us in the end. Love is contagious. Nothing is more edifying then receiving smiles and affirmations from someone else. It makse the soul feel good. You can experience the opposite through hate, but it's bad feelings we experience.

Duty makes us do things well, but love makes us do them beautifully. ~ Phillips Brooks

Always remember that today might be your last day on earth. Live today as if it were your last. ~Unknown

Hate is never ended be hatred but by love. ~ BUDDA

If you live to be a hundred, I want to live to be a hundred minus one day so I never have to live without you. ~A.A. Milne (Winnie-the-Pooh)

Love's a choice. Make wise decisions. ~Shellie R. Warren

Love has nothing to do with what you are expecting to get ~only with what you are expecting to give ~which is everything. ~Katharine Hepburn

The most important thing in any relationship is not what you get but what you give.... In any case, the giving of love is an education in itself. ~Eleanor Roosevelt

Beauty is in the eye of the beholder. ~Margaret Wolfe Hungerford

Everything has beauty, but not everyone sees it. ~Confucius

Beauty is not caused. It is. ~Emily Dickinson

What we see depends mainly on what we look for. ~Sir John Lubbock

We don't see things as they are, we see them as we are. ~Anais Nin

Love is the beauty of the soul. ~St. Augustine

Love is an attempt to change a piece of a dream world into reality. ~Theodor Reik

We cannot really love anybody with whom we never laugh. ~Agnes Repplier

What is most beautiful in virile men is something feminine; what is most beautiful in feminine women is something masculine. ~Susan Sontag

Love looks not with the eyes, but with the mind; And therefore is winged Cupid painted blind. ~William Shakespeare

A successful marriage requires falling in love many times, always with the same person. ~Mingon McLaughlin

Ultimately magic finds you, if you let it. ~Tony Wheeler

We only part to meet again. ~John Gay

In love there are two things: bodies and words. ~Joyce Carol Oates

Many things in life will catch your eye but few will catch your heart... Pursue those. ~Unknown

Knowledge is gained by learning; trust by doubt; skill by practice; and love by love. ~Thomas Szasz

Life has taught us that love does not consist in gazing at each other but in looking together in the same direction. ~Antoine de Saint-Exupery

When two people love each other, they don't look at each other, they look in the same direction. ~Ginger Rogers

Love cures people ~ both the ones who give it and the ones who receive it. ~Dr. Karl Menninger

Love only grows by sharing. You can only have more for yourself by giving it away to others. ~Brian Tracey

Two souls with a single thought, Two hearts that beat as one. ~Friedrich Halm Ingomar

The best proof of love is trust. ~Dr. Joyce Brothers

If you are in love...that's about the best thing that can happen to anyone. Don't let anyone make it small or light to you. ~John Steinbeck

Love is the but the discovery of ourselves in others and the delight in the recognition. ~Alexander Smith

Love is not blind - it sees more, not less. But because it sees more, it is willing to see less. ~Rabbi Julins Gordon

Some say love is blind while others say there is love at first sight. For those who say love is blind, I say open your eyes and take in the endless possibilities of beauty and compassion. For those who believe in love at first sight, take time to close your eyes, look into your heart, and find out whose face it is that you see. ~John S.

You aren't wealthy until you have something money can't buy. ~Garth Brooks

To write a good love letter, you ought to begin without knowing what you mean to say and to finish without knowing what you have written. ~Jean Jacques Rousseau

Love me when I least deserve it, because that's when I really need it. ~Swedish proverb

We love because it's the only true adventure. ~Nikki Giovanni

Love doesn't make the world go 'round, love is what makes the ride worthwhile. ~Franklin P. Adams

Love cures people ~ both the ones who give it and the ones who receive it. ~Dr. Karl Menninger

Age does not protect you from love. But love, to some extent, protects you from age. ~Anais Nin

If you admire someone instead of noticing the ways you don't measure up, notice the ways in which you are similar. We really admire only people who reflect an image of what we already know is the best in ourselves. Train yourself to see what is similar! ~unknown

Love those who love you while they are alive. ~Rael

Make sure that you let them know that you love them while you still have many years to go. ~Mason Ovian

Time goes by so fast, people go in and out of your life. You must never miss the opportunity to tell these people how much they mean to you. ~From the last episode of Cheers

Do not save your loving speeches for your friends till they are dead; Do not write them on their tombstones, speak them rather now instead. ~Anna Cummins

The way to love anything is to realize that it might be lost. ~G. K. Chesterton

Ever has it been that love knows not its own depth until the hour of separation. ~Khalil Gibran

One word frees us of all the weight and pain in life. That word is love. ~Sophocles

The relationship between commitment and doubt is by no means an antagonistic one. Commitment is healthiest when it is not without doubt but in spite of doubt. ~Rollo May

Love is an irresistable desire to be irresistably desired. ~Robert Frost

Young love is a flame; very pretty, often very hot and fierce, but still only light and flickering. The love of the older and disciplined heart is as coals, deep burning, unquenchable. ~Henry Ward Beecher

How many times does your heart meet...the most beautiful girl in the world? ~Harry Connick, Jr.

The sound of a kiss is not so loud as that of a cannon, but its echo lasts a great deal longer. ~Oliver Wendell Holmes

For it was not into my ear you whispered, but into my heart. It was not my lips you kissed, but my soul. ~Judy Garland

And now here is my secret, a very simple secret; it is only with the heart that one can see rightly, what is essential is invisible to the eye. ~Antoine de Saint-Exupéry

Love is not limited by convenience; it is the inconvenient times that make you realize how much you are truly loved. ~Officer Michael A. Mejia

I have no regrets. I will never regret loving someone because the feeling of love for five minutes is greater than an eternity of hurt. ~Kurt Langner

Among those whom I like or admire, I can find no common denominator, but among those whom I love, I can: all of them make me laugh. ~Wystan Hugh Auden

We women take love too seriously. Men wish to be loved with laughter, not with sighing. So laugh, sweetheart, laugh, or soon you may be weeping. ~Minna Thomas Antrim

Tis better to have loved and lost than never to have loved at all. ~Alfred Lord Tennyson

If I had a flower for every time I thought of you...I could walk through my garden forever.
~Alfred Lord Tennyson

Sometimes the heart sees whats invisble to the eye.—Alfred Lord Tennyson

Love is like the North Star. In a changing world, it's always constant. ~Gordon B. Hinckley

Love is meant to be an adventure! ~Gordon B. Hinckley

To the world you may be just one person, but to one person, you are the world. ~Unknown

Whatever you are, be a good one. ~Abraham Lincoln

Those who stand for nothing fall for anything. ~Alexander Hamilton

It's important that people should know what you stand for. It's equally important that they know what you won't stand for. ~Mary H. Waldrip

In matters of style, swim with the current, In matters of principle, stand like a rock. ~Thomas Jefferson

If you aren't good at loving yourself, you will have a difficult time loving anyone, since you'll resent the time and energy you give another person that you aren't even giving to yourself. ~Barbara de Angelis

Until you value yourself, you won't value your time. Until you value your time, you will not do anything with it. ~Dr. M. Scott Peck

Don't be afraid if things seem difficult in the beginning. That's only the initial impression. The important thing is not to retreat; you have to master yourself. ~Olga Korbut

The greatest of all faults is to be conscious of none. ~Thomas Carlyle

There is only one corner of the universe you can be certain of improving and that is your own self. ~Aldous Huxley

There's always room for improvement, you know ~it's the biggest room in the house. ~Louise Heath Leber

The greatest discovery of my generation is that human beings can alter their lives by altering their attitudes of mind. ~William James

I am a big believer in the 'mirror test. All that matters is if you can look in the mirror and honestly tell the person you see there, that you've done your best. ~John McKay

I count him braver who overcomes his desires than him who conquers his enemies; for the hardest victory is the victory over self. ~Aristotle

The experienced mountain climber is not intimidated by a mountain ~he is inspired by it. The persistent winner is not discouraged by a problem ~he is challenged by it. Mountains are created to be conquered; adversities are designed to be defeated; problems are sent to be solved. It is better to master one mountain than a thousand foothills. ~William Arthur Ward

You may be deceived if you trust too much, but you will live in torment if you do not trust enough. ~Frank Crane

I always prefer to believe the best of everybody – it saves so much trouble. ~Joseph Rudyard Kipling

Personality can open doors, but only character can keep them open. ~Elmer G. Letterman

Character is like a tree and reputation like its shadow. The shadow is what we think of it; the tree is the real thing. ~Abraham Lincoln

I have found that being honest is the best technique I can use. Right up front, tell people what you're trying to accomplish and what you're willing to sacrifice to accomplish it. ~Lee Iacocca

Knowing others is intelligence; knowing yourself is true wisdom. Mastering others is strength; mastering yourself is true power. If you realize that you have enough, you are truly rich. ~Tao Te Ching

At the end of our life, we ought to be able to look back over it from our deathbed and know somehow the world is a better place because we lived, we loved, we were other-centered, other-focused. ~Joe Erhmann

The key to happiness is having dreams. The key to success is making your dreams come true. ~ Anonymous

The lights of stars that were extinguished ages ago still reaches us. So it is with great men who died centuries ago, but still reach us with the radiations of their personalities. ~Khalil Gibran

It is only as we develop others that we permanently succeed. ~Harvey S. Firestone

A sense of humor is part of the art of leadership, of getting along with people, of getting things done."-Dwight D. Eisenhower

When the effective leader is finished with his work, the people say it happened naturally.Lao Tsu

The final test of a leader is that he leaves behind him in other men the conviction and the will to carry on. ~Walter Lippmann

Good leaders are like baseball umpires - they go practically unnoticed when doing their jobs right." ~Byrd Baggett

Leadership: The art of getting someone else to do something you want done because he wants to do it. ~Dwight D. Eisenhower

If you don't understand that you work for your mislabeled subordinates, then you know nothing of leadership. You know only tyranny. ~Dee W. Hock

Every great person is always being helped by everybody; for their gift is to get good out of all things and all persons. ~John Ruskin

Leaders think and talk about the solutions. Followers think and talk about the problems. ~Brian Tracey

No man will make a great leader who wants to do it all himself, or to get all the credit for doing it. ~Andrew Carnegie

The best executive is one who has sense enough to pick good people to do what he wants done, and self-restraint enough to keep from meddling with them while they do it. ~Theodore Roosevelt

The quality of a leader is reflected in the standards they set for themselves. ~Ray Kroc

Few things help an individual more than to place responsibility upon him, and to let him know that you trust him. ~Booker T. Washington

Management works in the system. Leadership works on the system. ~Stephen R. Covey

Good management consists of showing average people how to do the work of superior people. ~John D. Rockefeller

Outstanding leaders go out of their way to boost the self-esteem of their personnel. If people believe in themselves, it's amazing what they can accomplish. High expectations are the key to everything. ~Sam Walton

Keep away from people who try to belittle your ambition. Small people always do that, but the really great make you feel that you, too, can become great. ~Mark Twain

No person can be a great leader unless he takes genuine joy in the successes of those under him. ~W. H. Auden

Expect people to be better than they are; it helps them to become better. But don't be dissapointed when they're not; it helps them to keep trying. ~Merry Browne

If we treat people as they ought to be, we help them become what they are capable of becoming. ~Goethe

Many people take no care of their money till they come nearly to the end of it, and others do just the same with their time. ~Johann von Goethe

Treat people as if they were what they ought to be, and you help them to become what they are capable of being. ~Johann Wolfgang von Goethe

At the risk of seeming ridiculous, let me say that the true revolutionary is guided by a great feeling of love. It is impossible to think of a genuine revolutionary lacking this quality. ~ Che Guevera

In the final analysis, it is not what you do for your children but what you have taught them to do for themselves that will make them successful human beings. ~Ann Landers

Integrity is the most valuable and respected quality of leadership. Always keep your word. ~Brian Tracey

The challenge of leadership is to be strong, but not rude; be kind, but not weak; be bold, but not a bully; be thoughtful, but not lazy; be humble, but not timid; be proud, but not arrogant; have humor, but without folly. ~Jim Rohn

A superior man is modest in his speech, but exceeds in his actions. ~Confucius

If you raise your children to feel that they can accomplish any goal or task they decide upon, you will have succeeded as a parent and you will have given your children the greatest of all blessings. ~Brian Tracy

...do your homework. You can't lead without knowing what you're talking about... ~George Bush

Great men never make bad use of their superiority. They see it and feel it and are not less modest. The more they have, the more they know their own deficiencies. ~Jean Jacques Rousseau

The great are great only because we are on our knees. Let us rise! ~Max Stirner

Be not afraid of greatness; some are born great, some achieve greatness, and others have greatness thrust upon them. ~William Shakespeare

Great work is done by people who are not afraid to be great. ~Fernando Flores

Anybody who accepts mediocrity-in school, on the job, in life-is a person who compromises, and when the leader compromises, the whole organization compromises. ~Charles Knight

Children are educated by what the grown-up is and not by his talk." ~Carl Jung

PART III

I. Mind

The mind is ones most important characteristic of dictating one's actions. There is a three step process before one acts. One must first think of something, desire to do it, and then do the act. So if one wants to change a learned behavior the place to start is to change the thoughts within one's mind. If one controls what one thinks one can control one's desire which leads to controlling one's actions.

The soul is dyed the color of its thoughts. ~ Marcus Aurelius

If you are distressed by anything external, the pain is not due to the thing itself but to your own estimate of it; and this you have the power to revoke at any moment. ~Marcus Aurelius

He who has a firm will makes the world to himself. ~Goethe

There is nothing either good or bad but thinking makes it so. ~Shakespeare

I have had a great many troubles in my life, and most never happened.. ~ Mark Twain

All that we are is the result of what we have thought. ~Buddha

The mind is everything; what you think, you become. – Buddha

You are today where your thoughts have brought you. You will be tomorrow where your thoughts take you. – James Allen

We become what we think about. – Napoleon Hill

A man is what he thinks about all day long. – Ralph Waldo Emerson

Wherever you are, be there. - Ralph Waldo Emerson

As a man Thinketh in his heart, so is he – David, the psalmist

Mindfulness involves intentionally doing only one thing at a time and making sure I am here for it. ~ Jon Kabat-Zinn

Wherever you go, there you are - Kabat-Zinn

Love looks not with the eyes, but with the mind. ~William Shakespeare

II. Overcome the Fear to Risk

Taking risk and overcoming fear is what makes life enjoyable. If we didn't take risk we would never make opportunities to grow and learn. Fear is our greatest enemy and holds us back from reaching our potential. Everyone builds a comfort zone around themselves, and when they leave it they feel tension and apprehension. Though, the secret of life is to live outside this self build fence. To really enjoy life we must live more outside the fence then within. So do the things you fear doing and you will feel more alive than ever.

Be strong and of good courage, be not afraid, neither be thou dismayed: for the Lord thy God is with thee whither so ever thou goest. ~Joshua 1:9

I sought the Lord, and he heard me, and delivered me from all my fears. ~Psalms 34: 4

Yea, though I walk through the valley of the shadow of death, I will fear no evil: for thou art with me; thy rod and thy staff they comfort me. ~PSALM 23:4

One man with courage is a majority. ~Thomas Jefferson

All men have fears, but the brave put down their fears and go forward, sometimes to death, but always to victory. ~Greece King's Guard

Only those who dare to fail greatly can ever achieve greatly. ~Robert F. Kennedy

To win without risk is to triumph without glory. ~Pierre Corneille

I'd rather regret the things I have done than the things I have not. ~Lucille Ball

Show me a person who has never made a mistake and I'll show you somebody who has never achieved much. ~Joan Collins

We must dare, and dare again, and go on daring. ~Georges Jacques Danton

...the creator of the new composition in the arts is an outlaw until he is a classic. ~Gertrude Stein

A fool is someone whose pencil wears out before its eraser does. ~Marilyn vos Savant

He who never made a mistake, never made a discovery. ~Samuel Smiles

If you're not failing every now and again, it's a sign you're not doing anything very innovative. ~Woody

Allen Rejoice with joy unspeakable and full of glory. ~1 Peter 1:8

This is the day which the Lord hath made, rejoice and be glad. ~Psalms 118:24

Be strong and of good courage, be not afraid, neither be thou dismayed: for the Lord thy God is with thee whither so ever thou goest. Joshua 1:9

I sought the Lord, and he heard me, and delivered me from all my fears. Psalms 34: 4

If you are never scared, embarrassed, or hurt, it means you never take chances. ~Julia Soul

However well organized the foundations of life may be, life must always be full of risks. ~Havelock Ellis

If you're not making mistakes, you're not taking risks, and that means you're not going anywhere. The key is to make mistakes faster than the competition, so you have more changes to learn and win. ~John W. Holt, Jr.

Be bold. If you're going to make an error, make a doozy, and don't be afraid to hit the ball. ~Billie Jean King

Far better to dare mighty things, to win glorious triumphs, even though checkered by failure, than to take rank with those poor spirits who neither enjoy much nor suffer much, because they live in the gray twilight that knows not victory, nor defeat. ~Theodore Roosevelt

Of course we all have our limits, but how can you possibly find your boundaries unless you explore as far and as wide as you possibly can? I would rather fail in an attempt at something new and uncharted than safely succeed in a repeat of something I have done. ~A.E. Hotchner

And the trouble is, if you don't risk anything, you risk even more. ~Erica Jong

The greatest mistake you can make in life is to be continually fearing you will make one. ~Elbert Hubbard

Take chances, make mistakes. That's how you grow. Pain nourishes your courage. You have to fail in order to practice being brave. ~Mary Tyler Moore

Creativity is allowing oneself to make mistakes. Art is knowing which ones to keep. ~Scott Adams

Great deeds are usually wrought at great risks. ~Herodotus

I have missed more than 9,000 shots in my career. I have lost almost 300 games. On 26 occasions I have been entrusted to take the game winning shot...And I missed. And I have failed over and over and over again in my life. And that is precisely ... why I succeed. ~Michael Jordan

Every great advance in science has issued from a new audacity of imagination. ~John Dewey

To imagine is everything, to know is nothing at all. ~Anatole France

To know is nothing at all; to imagine is everything. ~Anatole France

Imagination is more important than knowledge. Knowledge is limited. Imagination encircles the world. ~Albert Einstein

Imagination is the beginning of creation. You imagine what you desire, you will what you imagine and at last you create what you will. ~George Bernard Shaw

Take a chance! All life is a chance. The man who goes furthest is generally the one who is willing to do and dare. The "sure thing" boat never gets far from shore. ~Dale Carnegie

Imagination is the spark that ignites the fire of creativity. ~Richard Laurence Peterson

All acts performed in the world begin in the imagination. ~Barbara Grizzuti Harrison

Sometimes you just have to take the leap, and build your wings on the way down. ~Kobi Yamada

I find the great thing in this world is not so much where we stand, as in what direction we are moving: To reach the port of heaven, we must sail sometimes with the wind and sometimes against it, but we must sail, and not drift, nor lie at anchor. ~Oliver Wendell Holmes, Jr.

He that will not sail till all dangers are over must never put to sea. ~Thomas Fuller

Every accomplishment starts with the decision to try. ~Anonymous

Procrastination is the fear of success. People procrastinate because they are afraid of the success that they know will result if they move ahead now. Because success is heavy, carries a responsibility with it, it is much easier to procrastinate and live on the "someday I'll" philosophy. ~Denis Waitley Everything we do has a result. But that which is right and prudent does not always lead to good, nor the contrary to what is bad. ~Goethe

If you wait for opportunities to occur, you will be one of the crowd. ~Edward de Bono

You can't cross the sea merely by staring at the water. ~Rabindranath Tagore

A ship in harbor is safe, But that is not what ships are built for. ~Unknown

Twenty years from now you will be disappointed by things you didn't do than by the ones you did do. So throw off the bowlines. Sail away from the safe harbor. Catch the trade winds in your sail. Explore. Dream. Discover. ~Mark Twain

Behold the turtle. He makes progress only when he sticks his neck out. ~James B. Conant

Don't be afraid to take a big step. You can't cross a chasm in two small jumps. ~David Lloyd George

No one ever became great by imitation. ~Samuel Johnson

Self-confidence is the result of a successfully survived risk. ~Jack Gibb

The minute you settle for less than you deserve, you get even less than you settled for. ~Maureen Dowd

Do not be too timid and squeamish about your actions. All life is an experiment. The more experiments you make the better. What if they are a little course and you may get your coat soiled or torn? What if you do fail, and get fairly rolled in the dirt once or twice. Up again, you shall never be so afraid of a tumble. ~Ralph Waldo Emerson

I want to stay as close to the edge as I can without going over. Out on the edge you see all kinds of things you can't see from the center. ~Kurt Vonnegut

People who are unable to motivate themselves must be content with mediocrity, no matter how impressive their other talents. ~Andrew Carnegie

If you're not big enough to lose, you're not big enough to win. ~Walter Reuntner

Any time you try to win everything, you must be willing to lose everything. ~Larry Csonka

Always do what you are afraid to do. ~Ralph Waldo

She didn't know it couldn't be done so she went ahead and did it. ~Mary's Almanac

Some things cannot be spoken or discovered until we have been stuck, incapacitated, or blown off course for awhile. Plain sailing is pleasant, but you are not going to explore many unknown realms that way. ~David Whyte

It's kind of fun to do the impossible. ~Walt Disney

A failure is like fertilizer; it stinks to be sure, but it makes things grow faster in the future. ~Dennis Waitley

My mother gave me a bumblebee pin when I started work. She said: 'Aerodynamically, bees shouldn't be able to fly. But they do. Remember that. ~Jill E. Barad

The greater the difficulty, the more glory in surmounting it. ~Epicurus

Never measure the height of a mountain until you have reached the top. Then you will see how low it was. ~Dag Hammarskjold

If everything seems under control, you're just not going fast enough. ~Mario Andretti

When you get to the end of your rope, tie a knot and hang on. ~Franklin D. Roosevelt

The reward of a thing well done is to have done it ~Ralph Waldo Emerson

We don't know who we are until we see what we can do. ~Martha Grimes

Nothing in this world is impossible to a willing heart. ~Abraham Lincoln

Much of the best work of the world has been done against seeming impossibilities. ~Dale Carnegie

In the long run, we get no more than we have been willing to risk giving. ~Sheldon Kopp

Why not go out on a limb? Isn't that where the fruit is? ~Frank Scully

The greatest pleasure in life is doing what people say you cannot do. ~Walter Bagehot Progress always involves risk; you can't steal second base and keep your foot on first. ~Frederick Wilcox

The trouble in America is not that we are making too many mistakes, but that we are making too few. ~Phil Knight

Failure seldom stops you. What stops you is the fear of failure. ~Jack Lemmon

Failure is an event, not a person. Yesterday ended last night. ~Zig Ziglar

Failure is an event, never a person. ~William D. Brown

We must build dikes of courage to hold back the flood of fear. ~Martin Luther King, Jr.

Commit yourself to a dream. Nobody who tries to do something great but fails is a total failure. Why? Because he can always rest assured that he succeeded in life's most important battle - he defeated the fear of trying. ~Robert Schuller

The fear of becoming a 'has-been' keeps some people from becoming anything. ~Eric Hoffer

Destiny is not a matter of chance, it is a matter of choice; it is not a thing to be waited for, it is a thing to be achieved. ~William Jennings Bryan

It's not your blue blood, your pedigree or your college degree. It's what you do with your life that counts. ~Millard Fuller

Set your sights high, the higher the better. Expect the most wonderful things to happen, not in the future but right now. Realize that nothing is too good. Allow absolutely nothing to hamper you or hold you up in any way. ~Eileen Caddy

Don't worry about being successful. Worry about being significant. ~Oprah Winfrey

Far away there in the sunshine are my highest aspirations. I may not reach them, but I can look up and see their beauty, believe in them, and try to follow where they lead. ~Louisa May Alcott

Make the most of yourself...for that is all there is of you. ~Ralph Waldo Emerson

Always dream and shoot higher than you know how to. Don't bother just to be better than your contemporaries or predecessors. Try to be better than yourself. ~William Faulkner

I dream, therefore I become. ~Cheryl Grossman

As long as you're going to think anyway, think big. ~Donald Trump

The greater danger for most of us is not that our aim is too high and we miss it, but that it is too low and we reach it. ~Michelangelo

You are never given a dream without also being given the power to make it true. ~Unknown

Your hopes, dreams and aspirations are legitimate. They are trying to take you airborne, above the clouds, above the storms, if you only let them. ~William James

My interest is in the future because I am going to spend the rest of my life there. ~Charles F. Kettering

To laugh is to risk appearing the fool.
To weep is to risk appearing sentimental.
To reach for another is to risk involvement.
To expose your feelings is to risk exposing your true self.
To place your ideas, your dreams before a crowd is to risk their loss.
To love is to risk not being loved in return.
To live is to risk dying.
To believe is to risk despair.
To try is to risk failure.
But risks must be taken, because the greatest hazard in life is to risk nothing. The person who risks nothing, does nothing, has nothing, is nothing. They may avoid suffering and sorrow, but they cannot learn, feel, change, grow, love, live. Chained by their attitudes they are slaves; they have forfeited their freedom. Only a person who risks is free.

~Anonymous Chicago teacher (Ralph Waldo Emerson?)

III. Philosophers

If you look into your own heart, and you find nothing wrong there, what is there to worry about? What is there to fear? ~Confucius

He who learns but does not think, is lost! He who thinks but does not learn is in great danger. ~Confucius

I hear and I forget. I see and I remember. I do and I understand. ~Confucius

The superior man is satisfied and composed; the mean man is always full of distress. ~Confucius

What the superior man seeks is in himself; what the small man seeks is in others. ~Confucius

"Don't complain about the snow on your neighbor's roof, "Said Confuses, "when your own doorstep is unclean."

Choose a job you love, and you will never have to work a day in your life.
~Confucius

The only people who cannot change are the most wise and the most stupid. ~Confucius

Only the wisest and the stupidest of men never change. ~Confucius

The people may be made to follow a path of action, but they may not be made to understand it. ~Confucius

Everything has beauty, but not everyone sees it. ~Confucius

The diamond cannot be polished without friction, not man perfected without trials. ~Confucius

Our greatest glory is not in never falling, but in rising every time we fall. ~Confucius

A superior man is modest in his speech, but exceeds in his actions. ~Confucius

To know what is right and not to do it is the worst cowardice. ~Confucius

A thousand-mile journey begins with a single step. ~Lao-Tzu

When you are content to be simply yourself and don't compare or compete, everybody will respect you. ~Lao Tzu

When the effective leader is finished with his work, the people say it happened naturally. ~Lao Tzu

What is a friend? A single soul dwelling in two bodies. ~Aristotle

Those who cannot bravely face danger are the slaves of their attackers. ~Aristotle

Those who cannot bravely face danger are the slaves of their attackers. ~Aristotle

We are what we repeatedly do. Excellence then is not an act but a habit. ~Aristotle

I count him braver who overcomes his desires than him who conquers his enemies; for the hardest victory is the victory over self. ~Aristotle

Those who cannot bravely face danger are the slaves of their attackers. ~Aristotle

Those who cannot bravely face danger are the slaves of their attackers. ~Aristotle

Education is the best provision for the journey to old age. ~Aristotle

It is unbecoming for young men to utter maxims. ~Aristotle

Law is mind without reason. ~Aristotle

Pleasure in the job put perfection in the work. ~Aristotle

Poverty is the parent of revolution and crime. ~Aristotle

To perceive is to suffer. ~Aristotle

It is not always the same thing to be a good man and a good citizen. ~Aristotle

For the things we have to learn before we can do them, we learn by doing them. ~Aristotle

One swallow does not make a summer. ~Aristotle

To him who is afraid, everything rustles. ~Sophocles

Brave hearts do not back down. ~Sophocles

To him who is afraid, everything rustles. ~Sophocles

Brave hearts do not back down. ~Sophocles

Fortune and love favor the brave. ~Ovid

One thing only I know, and that is that I know nothing. Socrates

He who has a firm will makes the world to himself.~Goethe

Every second is of infinite value. ~Johann Wolfgang von Goethe

Be kind, for everyone you meet is fighting a hard battle. ~Plato

Necessity is the mother of invention. ~Plato

The spiritual eyesight improves as the physical eyesight declines. ~Plato

He who is of a calm and happy nature will hardly feel the pressure of age, but to him who is of an opposite disposition, youth and age are equally a burden. ~Plato

Science is nothing but perception. ~Plato

Knowledge which is acquired under compulsion has no hold on the mind. Therefore do not use compulsion, but let early education be rather a sort of amusement; this will better enable you to find out the natural bent of the child. ~Plato

We are twice armed if we fight with faith. ~Plato

Wise people talk because they have something to say; fools, because they have to say something. ~Plato

The punishment which the wise suffer, who refuse to take part in government, is to live under the government of worse men. ~Plato

One of the penalties for refusing to participate in politics is that you end up being governed by your inferiors. ~Plato

Those who are too smart to engage in politics are punished by being governed by those who are dumber. ~Plato

It is as expedient that a wicked man be punished as that a sick man be cured by a physician; for all chastisement is a kind of medicine. ~Plato

You can learn more about a person in an hour of play than you can from a lifetime of conversation. ~Plato

Ignorance is the root and stem of every evil. ~Plato

Let parents then bequeath to their children not riches but the spirit of reverence. ~Plato

Education is teaching our children to desire the right things. ~Plato

The direction in which education starts a man will determine his future life. ~Plato

For a man to conquer himself is the first and noblest of all victories. ~Plato

Knowledge which is acquired under compulsion has no hold on the mind. Therefore do not use compulsion, but let early education be rather a sort of amusement; this will better enable you to find out the natural bent of the child. ~Plato

The object of education is to teach us to love what is beautiful. ~Plato

You can discover more about a person in an hour of play than in a year of conversation. – Plato

IV. The Fight

That which we persist in doing becomes easier—not that the nature of the thing has changed, but that our ability to do it has increased. ~Heber J. Grant

A man is not finished when he is defeated. He is finished when he quits. ~Richard [Milhous] Nixon

Without a struggle, there can be no progress. ~Frederick Douglass

Great things are not done by impulse, but by a series of small things brought together. ~Vincent Van Gogh

We cannot all do great things, but we can do small things with great love. ~Mother Teresa

You never really lose until you quit trying. ~Mike Ditka

If you cannot do great things yourself, remember that you may do small things in a great way. ~Swamy Chinmayananda

You are not beaten until you admit it. ~George S. Patton, Jr

A quitter never wins and a winner never quits. ~Napoleon Hill

They say it can't be done, but that doesn't always work. ~Casey Stengel

Little things affect little minds. ~Benjamin Disraeli

If you don't quit, and don't cheat, and don't run home when trouble arrives, you can only win. ~Shelley Long

Nobody trips over mountains. It is the small pebble that causes you to stumble. Pass all the pebbles in your path and you will find you have crossed the mountain. ~Unknown

If you're trying to achieve, there will be roadblocks. I've had them; everybody has had them. But obstacles don't have to stop you. If you run into a wall, don't turn around and give up. Figure out how to climb it, go through it, or work around it. ~Michael Jordan

Patience and perseverance have a magical effect before which difficulties disappear and obstacles vanish. ~John Quincy Adams

Great minds have purposes; little minds have wishes. Little minds are subdued by misfortunes; great minds rise above them. ~Washington Irving

Let me tell you the secret that has led me to my goal: my strength lies solely in my tenacity. ~Louis Pasteur

Anything worth having has its price. ~Joan Didion

A somebody was once a nobody who wanted to and did. ~Unknown

Do it first, do it yourself, and keep on doin' it. ~Ben Hecht

You can't build a reputation on what you are going to do. ~Henry Ford

There is no security on this earth, there is only opportunity. ~Douglas MacArthur

You miss 100 percent of the shots you never take. ~Wayne Gretzky

Opportunities are never lost. The other fellow takes those you miss. ~Anonymous

Four things come not back: the spoken word, the spent arrow, the past, the neglected opportunity. ~Omar Idn Al-Halif

Things may come to those who wait, but only the things left by those who hustle. ~Abraham Lincoln

Fortune knocks but once, but misfortune has much more patience. ~Laurence J. Peter

The bitterest tears shed over graves are for words left unsaid and deeds left undone. ~Harriet Beecher Stowe

Regret for wasted time is more wasted time. ~Mason Cooley

Whatever you want to do, do it now! There are only so many tomorrows. ~Michael Landon

The sad truth is that opportunity doesn't knock twice. You can put things off until tomorrow but tomorrow may never come. ~Gloria Estefan

Don't sit down and wait for the opportunities to come; you have to get up and make them. ~Madame C. J. Walker

Don’t stand around and wait for something to happen. Don’t be afraid to take chances. Gamble. Be reckless. Make things happen! ~Joe Paterno

Do not wait; the time will never be "just right." Start where you stand, and work with whatever tools you may have at your command, and better tools will be found as you go along. ~Napoleon Hill

How you spend your time defines who you are. ~Oprah Winfrey

A wise man will make more opportunities than he finds. ~Francis Bacon

Nothing is so irretrievably missed as an opportunity we encounter every day. ~Marie Von Ebner-Eschenbach

Wish you were more daring. Stop pining and take the plunge. Pick something you really want to accomplish and go for it. ~Unknown

The idle man does not know what it is to enjoy rest. ~Albert Einstein

I don’t' think necessity is the mother of invention ~ invention, in my opinion, arise directly from idleness, possibly also from laziness. To save oneself trouble." ~Agatha Christie

Ability is nothing without opportunity. ~Napoleon Bonaparte

You put out, boy, you suck up your gut, give it all you’ve got and you give me that second effort. You give me that much boy...and I’ll show you glory. ~Paul “Bear” Bryant

One of the strongest characteristics of genius is the power of lighting its own fire. ~John W. Foster

I can accept failure. Everyone fails at something. But I can't accept not trying. ~Michael Jordan

I can accept anything, except what seems to be the easiest for most people: the half-way, the almost, the just-about, the in-between. ~Ayn Rand

Even if you're on the right track, you'll get run over if you just sit there. ~Will Rogers

Thou shalt not be a victim. Thou shalt not be a perpetrator. Above all, thou shalt not be a bystander. ~Holocaust Museum, Washington, DC

You may be disappointed if you fail, but you are doomed if you don't try. ~Beverly Sills

No one knows what he can do until he tries. ~unknown

Nobody makes a greater mistake than he who did nothing because he could only do a little. ~Edmund Burke

In any moment of decision the best thing you can do is the right thing, the next best thing is the wrong thing, and the worst thing you can do is nothing. ~Theodore Roosevelt

There are costs and risks to a program of action, but they are far less than the long-range risks and costs of comfortable inaction. ~John F. Kennedy

Try not. Do or do not. There is no try. ~Yoda

Walk on road, hmm? Walk right side, safe. Walk left side, safe. Walk middle, sooner or later... get squished just like grape. Here karate same thing. Either you karate do, yes...or karate do, no. You karate do, 'guess so' ~ just like grape. Understand? ~Mr. Miyagi

There are no such things as excuses. There are reasons that why a particular decision was reached, and why that decision was not a good one. There is a discernible path that can be followed to find the reasons why a failure occurred. There are no excuses, only wrong decisions. ~Andy Hutchison

It is common sense to take a method and try it. If it fails, admit it frankly and try another. But above all, try something. ~Franklin D. Roosevelt

If you want something badly enough, make an attempt. If you want to paint, get a brush and do it. If you want to sing, sing. A lot of people get scared. They're afraid to fail. Take that word out of your vocabulary. You don't "fail." You've "tried your best. ~Jane Seymour

To try and fail is at least to learn. To fail to try is to suffer the loss of what might have been. ~Ben Franklin

A thousand-mile journey begins with a single step. ~Lao-Tzu

A year from now you may wish you had started today. ~Karen Lamb

Knowing is not enough; we must apply. Willing is not enough; we must do. ~Goethe

The time is always right to do what is right. ~Martin Luther King Jr

You will never 'find' time for anything. If you want time you must make it. ~Charles Buxton

In order to make your dreams come true, you must awaken and take charge. ~Natasha Newsome

So many of our dreams at first seem impossible, then they seem improbable, and then, when we summon the will, they soon become inevitable. ~Christopher Reeve

Dost thou love life? Then do not squander time for that's the stuff life is made of. ~Benjamin Franklin

Do not squander time, for that is the stuff life is made of. ~Benjamin Franklin

Know the true value of time; snatch, seize and enjoy every moment of it. No idleness...never put off till tomorrow what you can do today. ~Lord Chesterfield

A man would do nothing, if he waited until he could do it so well that no one would find fault with what he has done. ~John Henry Cardinal Newman

The first man gets the oyster, the second man gets the shell. ~Andrew Carnegie

I sometimes say that success just happens. That's not true. You have to make it happen. When I make up my mind to do something, I make sure it happens. You can't wait for the phone to ring. You have to ring them. ~Lord (Lew) Grade

Start living now. Stop saving the good china for that special occasion. Stop withholding your love until that special person materializes. Every day you are alive is a special occasion. Every minute, every breath, is a gift from God. ~Mary Manin Morrissey

"Time is more valuable than money. You can get more money, but you cannot get more time." ~Jim Rohn

Being busy does not always mean real work. The object of all work is production or accomplishment and to either of these ends there must be forethought, system, planning, intelligence, and honest purpose, as well as perspiration. Seeming to do is not doing. ~Thomas Edison

In the morning, I say: 'What is my exciting thing for today?'...Don't ask me about tomorrow. ~Barbara Jordan

Let's suppose you had a bank that each morning credited your account with $ 1,440 with one condition, whatever part of the $1,440 you had failed to use during the day would be erased from your account and no balance carried over...What would you do? Of course you'd draw out every cent, everyday and use it to your best advantage...Well, you have such a bank and its name is TIME. Every morning the bank credits you with 1,440 minutes. It writes off forever whatever portion you failed to invest to a good purpose... INVEST WISELY! ~Unknown

Guard well your spare moments. They are like uncut diamonds. Discard them and their value will never be known. Improve them and they will become the brightest gems in a useful life. ~Ralph Waldo Emerson

Most of us think having a list of priorities is a sign of a motivated, serious person. But there is one essential flaw in this perspective. We are not guaranteed a future; and even if we were we could not live in it. All we have is now. ~George Lawrence-Ell

Through perserverence many people win success out of what seemed destined to be certain failure. ~Benjamin Disraeli

Be of good cheer. Do not think of today's failures, but of the success that may come tomorrow. You have set yourself a difficult task, but you will succeed if you persevere; and you will find a joy in overcoming obstacles. ~Helen Keller

Success is not final, failure is not fatal: it is the courage to continue that counts. ~Winston Churchill

It ain't over till it's over. ~Yoga Berra

Life is a series of experiences, each of which makes us bigger, even though it is hard to realize this. For the world was built to develop character, and we must learn that the setbacks and griefs which we endure help us in our marching onward. ~Henry Ford

Surmounting difficulty is the crucible that forms character. ~Anthony Robbins

The soul would have no rainbow had the eyes no tears. ~John Vance Cheney

The way I see it, if you want the rainbow, you gotta put up with the rain. ~Dolly Parton

If you weep because the sun has set, your own tears will never let you see the stars. ~Hindu Proverb

The diamond cannot be polished without friction, not man perfected without trials. ~Confucius

Our greatest glory is not in never falling, but in rising every time we fall. ~Confucius

If we had no winter, the spring would not be so pleasant: if we did not sometimes taste of adversity, prosperity would not be so welcome. ~Anne Bradstreet

The best way out is always through. ~Robert Frost

Although the world is full of suffering, it is full also of the overcoming of it. ~Helen Keller

Sometimes being pushed to the wall gives you the momentum necessary to get over it. ~Peter de Jager

We cannot lead a choiceless life. Every day, every moment, every second, there is a choice. If it were not so, we would not be individuals. ~Ernest Holmes

If you can't sleep, then get up and do something instead of lying there worrying. It's the worry that gets you, not the lack of sleep. ~Dale Carnegie

Time is relative; its only worth depends upon what we do as it is passing. ~Albert Einstein

Time is the most valuable coin in your life. You and you alone will determine how that coin will be spent. Be careful that you do not let other people spend it for you. ~Carl Sandberg

Time is the coin of your life. It is the only coin you have, and only you can determine how it will be spent. Be careful lest you let other people spend it for you. ~Carl Sandburg

Keep on going and the chances are that you will stumble on something, perhaps when you are least expecting it. I have never heard of anyone stumbling on something sitting down. ~Charles F. Kettering

There is no scarcity of opportunity to make a living at what you love; there's only a scarcity of resolve to make it happen. ~Wayne W. Dyer

It is no use saying, 'We are doing our best.' You have got to succeed in doing what is necessary. ~Winston Churchill

The only habits you never conquer are the ones you put off doing something about. ~Wess Roberts

You must do the thing you think you cannot do. ~Eleanor Roosevelt

Never mistake motion for action. ~Ernest Hemmingway

History has demonstrated that the most notable winners usually encountered heartbreaking obstacles before they triumphed. They won because they refused to become discouraged by their defeats. ~Bertie Charles Forbes

Dream is the spark of passion; talent is the firework of its expression; perseverance, the sacred fire of its accomplishment. ~Daniel Chabot

Time is the longest distance between two places. ~Tennesse Williams

What you do speaks so loud that I cannot hear what you say. ~Ralph Waldo Emerson

Use what talents you possess; the woods would be very silent if no birds sang except those that sang best. ~Henry Van Dyke

We don't have an eternity to realize our dreams, only the time we are here. ~Susan Taylor

Destiny is not a matter of chance, it is a matter of choice; it is not a thing to be waited for, it is a thing to be achieved. ~William Jennings Bryan

"You can't just sit there and wait for people to give you that golden dream; you've got to get out there and make it happen for yourself. ~Diana Ross

The most practical, beautiful, workable philosophy in the world won't work ~if you won't. ~Zig Ziglar

I found out that the things that hurt us the most can become the fuel and the catalyst that propel us toward our destiny. It will either make you bitter or it will make you better. ~T.D. Jakes

Greatness is not in where we stand, but in what direction we are moving. We must sail sometimes with the wind and sometimes against it but sail we must, and not drift, nor lie at anchor. ~Oliver Wendell Holmes

Honest disagreement is often a good sign of progress. ~Mohandas K. Ghandi

The deeper that sorrow carves into your being, the more joy you can contain. ~Kahlil Gibran

Some people are always grumbling that roses have thorns. I am thankful that thorns have roses. ~Alphonse Karr

You can complain because roses have thorns, or you can rejoice because thorns have roses. ~Ziggy

Sometimes you have to get to rock bottom in order to see the right way back up." ~Kate Bell

"Some of us think holding on makes us strong; but sometimes it is letting go. ~Herman Hesse

When we long for life without difficulties, remind us that oaks grow strong in contrary winds and diamonds are made under pressure. ~Peter Marshall

The sea is dangerous and its storms terrible, but these obstacles have never been sufficient reason to remain ashore...unlike the mediocre, intrepid spirits seek victory over those things that seem impossible...it is with an iron will that they embark on the most daring of all endeavors...to meet the shadowy future without fear and conquer the unknown. ~Ferdinand Magellan

The willow knows what the storm does not: that the power to endure harm outlives the power to inflict it. ~Blood of the Martyr

You cannot prevent the birds of sorrow from flying over your head, but you can prevent them from building nests in your hair. ~Chinese Proverb

Usually when people are sad, they don't do anything. They just cry over their condition. But when they get angry, they bring about a change. ~Malcolm X

Remember all of us has problems we all have to deal with, so even though, you can't control what happens on the outside, you can control what happens on the inside. ~Unknown

Growing is a lifetime job, and we grow most when we're down in the valleys, where the fertilizer is. ~Barbara Johnson

In every job, relationship, or life situation there is inevitably some turbulence. Learn to laugh at it. It is part of what you do and who you are. ~Allen Klein

"The marvelous richness of human experience would lose something of rewarding joy if there were no limitations to overcome. The hilltop hour would not be half so wonderful if there were no dark valleys to traverse. ~Helen Keller

We could never learn to be brave and patient if there were only joy in the world." ~Helen Keller

Optimism is the faith that leads to achievement. Nothing can be done without hope and confidence. ~Helen Keller

When one door of happiness closes, another opens; but often we look so long at the closed door that we do not see the one which has opened for us. ~Helen Keller

Keep your face to the sunshine and you cannot see the shadow. ~Helen Keller

Over every mountain there is a path, although it may not be seen from the valley. ~James Rogers

Look for the light behind every shadow. ~Robert Schuler

Nobody really cares if you're miserable, so you might as well be happy. ~Cynthia Nelms

Flying may not be all plain sailing, but the fun of it is worth the price. ~Amelia Earhart

Faith is taking the first step even when you don't see the whole staircase. ~Martin Luther King Jr.

The ultimate measure of a man is not where he stands in moments of comfort, but where he stands at times of challenge and controversy. ~Martin Luther King, Jr.

We must accept finite disappointment, but never lose infinite hope. ~Martin Luther King Jr.

Take the first step in faith. You don't have to see the whole staircase, just take the first step. ~Martin Luther King Jr.

In doing anything, the first step is the most difficult. ~Chinese proverb

All things are difficult before they are easy. ~Thomas Fuller

Good timber does not grow with ease; The stronger the wind, the stronger the trees. ~J. Willard Marriott

Spend eighty percent of your time focusing on the opportunities of tomorrow rather than the problems of yesterday. ~Brian Tracey

Don't let life discourage you; everyone who got where he is had to begin where he was. ~Richard L. Evans

Success is how high you bounce when you hit bottom. ~General George Patton

Laughter gives us distance. It allows us to step back from an event, deal with it and then move on. ~Bob Newhart

Yesterday is not ours to recover, but tomorrow is ours to win or lose. ~Lyndon B. Johnson

Make the most of your regrets. To regret deeply is to live afresh. ~Henry David Thoreau

You have within you right now, everything you need to deal with whatever the world can throw at you. ~Brian Tracy

Truly, it is in darkness that one finds the light, so when we are in sorrow, then this light is nearest to all of us. ~Meister Eckhart

Fear can hold you prisoner, hope can set you free. ~Unknown

In difficult times, people too often lose the ability to face the future optimistically. They begin to think about their tomorrow's negatively. They forget that the tough times will pass. They concentrate on the problems of today rather than on the opportunities of tomorrow. In so doing, they not only lose the potential of today, they also throw away the beauty of tomorrow. ~Robert H. Schuller

I have had many troubles in my life, but the worst of them never came. ~James A. Garfield

Let us be of good cheer, remembering that the misfortunes hardest to bear are those which will never happen. ~James Russel Lowell

Make it a rule of life never to regret and never to look back. Regret is an appalling waste of energy, you can't build on it it's only good for wallowing in. ~Katherine Mansfield

There is not enough darkness in all the world to put out the light of even one small candle. ~Robert Alden

I have a duty to speak the truth as I see it and to share not just my triumphs, not just the things that felt good, but the pain, the intense, often unmitigating pain. It is important to share how I know survival is survival and not just a walk through the rain. ~Audre Lorde

V. Warriors

In war there is no substitute for victory. ~Gen. Douglas McArthur

All men have fears, but the brave put down their fears and go forward, sometimes to death, but always to victory. ~ Greece King's Guard

What counts is not necessarily the size of the dog in the fight - it's the size of the fight in the dog. ~Dwight D. Eisenhower

The most potent weapon in the hands of the oppressor is the mind of the oppressed. ~Steve Biko

Champions aren't made in gyms. Champions are made from something they have deep inside them - a desire, a dream, a vision. They have to have last-minute stamina, they have to be a little faster, they have to have the skill and the will. But the will must be stronger than the skill. ~Muhammad Ali

'Veni, vidi, vici' (I came, I saw, I conquered) ~Julius Caesar

The difference between the impossible and the possible lies in determination. ~Tommy Lasorda

There are not fifty ways of fighting, there is only one: to be the conqueror. ~Andre Malraux

Merit begets confidence, confidence begets enthusiasm, enthusiasm conquers the world. ~Walter H. Cottingham

"Man is made or unmade by himself; in the armory of thought he forges the weapons by which he destroys himself. He also fashions the tools with which he builds for himself heavenly mansions of joy and strength and peace. By the right choice and true application of thought, man ascends to the Divine Perfection; by the abuse and wrong application of thought, he descends below the level of the beast. Between these two extremes are all the grades of character, and man is their maker and master. ~James Allen

I have nothing to offer but blood, toil, tears and sweat. ~Winston S. Churchill

VI. Willingness to Change and Improve

You change your life by changing your heart. ~Max Lucado

It is not necessary to change. Survival is not mandatory. ~W. Edward Deming

Clinging to the past is the problem. Embracing change is the answer. ~Gloria Steinem

fears change. He feels security in the status quo, and he has an almost morbid fear of the new. For him, the greatest pain is the pain of a new idea. ~Martin Luther King Jr.

You must be the change you wish to see in the world. ~Mahatma Gandhi

What single ability do we all have? The ability to change. ~Leonard Andrews

It takes a deep commitment to change and an even deeper commitment to grow. ~Ralph Ellison

When we are no longer able to change a situation ... we are challenged to change ourselves. ~Victor Frankl

A scholar who cherishes the love of comfort is not fit to be deemed a scholar. ~Lao-Tzu

The chains of habit are too weak to be felt until they are too strong to be broken. ~Samuel Johnson

An elephant can be tethered by a thread ~if he believes he is captive. If we believe we are chained by habit or anxiety, we are in bondage. ~John H. Crowe

The man who views life at 50 the same as he did at 20 has wasted 30 years of his life. ~Muhammed Ali

The soft-minded man always The world moves and ideas that were good once are not always good. ~Eisenhower

Change doesn't happen while you're sitting around. Put your body in motion, and put your mind on alert that you plan to be proactive about your life from now on. ~Unknown

We cannot become what we need to be by remaining what we are. ~Max Depree

If we don't change, we don't grow. If we don't grow, we are not really living. ~Gail Sheehy

There are two kinds of people: those who are changing and those who are setting themselves up to be victims of change. As the world continues to march on around us, if I am only maintaining the status quo --if I'm not growing --then I'm falling behind. ~Jim Clemmer

You cannot expect to achieve new goals or move beyond your present circumstances unless you change. ~Les Brown

Truly every new idea is a violation of some older idea; as the awakening of tomorrow is a violation of today's slumber. As long as man continues to evolve, in other words, to separate himself from chaos, and to express himself in a higher form, he must always shatter something. In shattering, he disobeys: in breaking, he creates. ~Jeanne de Vietinghoff

To be successful one must make change an ongoing process. Quality is a race with no finish line. ~David T. Kearns

The important thing is this: to be able at any moment to sacrifice what we are for what we could become. ~Charles Du Bos

To be able to look at change as an opportunity to grow ~that is the secret to being happy. ~Joan Lunden

Instead of having the rug pulled from under your feet, learn to dance on a shifting carpet. ~Thomas F. Crum

Progress is a tide. If we stand still we will surely be drowned. To stay on the crest, we have to keep moving. ~Harold Mayfield

We are not retreating - we are advancing in another direction. ~General Douglas MacArthur

Only the wisest and the stupidest of men never change. ~Confucius

We are taught you must blame your father, your sisters, your brothers, the school, the teachers ~ you can blame anyone but never blame yourself. It's never your fault. But it's always your fault, because if you wanted to change, you're the one who has got to change. It's as simple as that, isn't it? ~Katherine Hepburn

A bore is someone who persists in holding his own views after we have enlightened him with ours. ~Unknown

A bore is a man who, when you ask him how he is, tells you. ~Bert Leston Taylor

People don't realize how a man's whole life can be changed by one book. ~Malcolm X

That's the risk you take if you change: that people you've been involved with won't like the new you. But other people who do will come along. ~Lisa Alther

Change means movement. Movement means friction. ~Saul Alinsky

If you never budge, don't expect a push. ~Malcolm Forbes

Do not consider painful what is good for you. ~Euripides

Where have you been the past five years, and if you don't make a change in your pattern where do you see yourself five years from now. ~Unknown

An error doesn't become a mistake until you refuse to correct it. ~Orlando A. Battista

The only people who cannot change are the most wise and the most stupid. ~Confucius

No man ever steps in the same river twice, for it's not the same river and he's not the same man. ~Heraclitus

…that a religion that does not require the sacrifice of all things never has power sufficient to produce the faith necessary unto life and salvation. ~Joseph Smith Jr.

VII. Willingness to Learn

When the pupil is ready the teacher will appear. ~Native American Saying

Teachers open the door, but you must enter by yourself. ~Chinese proverb

What was the duty of the teacher if not to inspire? ~Bharati Mukhejee

A teacher affects eternity: he can never tell where his influence stops. ~Henry Adams

The test of a good teacher is not how many questions he can ask his pupils that they will answer readily, but how many questions he inspires them to ask him which he finds it hard to answer. ~Alice Wellington Rollins

Good teaching is one-fourth preparation and three-fourths pure theatre. ~Gail Godwin

The aim of education is the knowledge, not of facts, but of values. ~William Ralph Inge

The goal of education is the advancement of knowledge and the dissemination of truth. ~President Kennedy

Education isn't a result. It's a process. ~Pierce Brosnan

Teaching should be such that what is offered is perceived as a valuable gift and not as a hard duty. ~Albert Einstein

Education is what remains after one has forgotten everything he learned in school. ~Albert Einstein

Iron rusts from disuse, stagnant water loses its purity, and in cold weather becomes frozen: even so does inaction sap the vigors of the mind. ~Leonardo da Vinci

Change does not necessarily assure progress, but progress implacably requires change. Education is essential to change, for education creates both new wants and the ability to satisfy them. ~Henry Steele Commager

Education is an important element in the struggle for human rights. It is the means to help our children and thereby increase self-respect. Education is our passport to the future, for tomorrow belongs to the people who prepare for it today. ~Malcolm X

The direction in which education starts a man will determine his future life. ~Plato

Education is not the filling of a pail, but the lighting of a fire. ~William Butler Yates

Education's purpose is to replace an empty mind with an open one. ~Malcolm S. Forbes

Anyone who stops learning is old, whether at twenty or eighty. Anyone who keeps learning stays young. The greatest thing in life is to keep your mind young. ~Henry Ford

A mind that has been stretched will never return to its original dimension. ~Albert Einstein

Commit yourself to lifelong learning. The most valuable asset you'll ever have is your mind and what you put into it. ~Brian Tracey

We encounter the grinding wheels that sharpen our mental blades many places in life. Adversity, school, parents, spiritual guides, books, experience are all sharpening teachers. As we grow older, to stay sharp we must find new grindstones to whet and sharpen our potential and keep us at our brightest, most penetrating best. ~Robert Kall

Too often we give our children answers to remember rather than problems to solve. ~Roger Lewin

Children enter school as question marks and leave as periods. ~Neil Postman

We cannot always build the future for our youth, but we can build our youth for the future. ~Franklin D. Roosevelt

Our children are our only hope for the future, but we are their only hope for their present and their future. ~Zig Ziglar

If you are planning for a year, sow rice; if you are planning for a decade, plant trees; if you are planning for a lifetime, educate people. ~Chinese proverb

Character development is the great, if not the sole, aim of education. ~O'Shea

VIII. Wisdom

If we look for human frailty in humans we will always find it. We live in a world where finding fault is the norm. ~Henry B. Eyring

God grant me the serenity to accept the things I cannot change, the courage to change the things I can, and the wisdom to know the difference. ~Reinhold Niebuhr

Content makes poor men rich; discontent makes rich men poor. - Benjamin Franklin

Any fool can criticize, condemn, and complain, and most fools do. ~Benjamin Franklin

Time is really the only capital that any human being has, and the only thing he can't afford to lose. ~Thomas Edison

Keep away from people who try to belittle your ambitions. Small people always do that, but the really great make you feel that you, too, can become great. ~Mark Twain

The stroke of the whip maketh marks in the flesh, but the stroke of the tongue breaketh the bones. ~Apocrypha

Those that fail to learn from history, are doomed to repeat it. ~Winston S. Churchill

When I have a little money, I buy books; and if I have any left, I buy food and clothes. ~Desiderius Erasmus Roterodamus

I know of no other practice which will make one more attractive in conversation than to be well-read in a variety of subjects. There is a great potential within each of us to go on learning. Regardless of our age, unless there be serious illness, we can read, study, drink in the writings of wonderful men and women. It is never too late to learn. ~Gordon B. Hinckley

There is something almost sacred about a great library because it represents the preservation of the wisdom, the learning, and the pondering of men and women of all the ages accumulated under one roof. ~Gordon B. Hinckley

Without books the development of civilization would have been impossible. They are the engines of change, windows on the world, "Lighthouses" as the poet said "erected in the sea of time." They are companions, teachers, magicians, bankers of the treasures of the mind, Books are humanity in print."
~Arthur Schopenhauer

Sometimes you earn more by doing jobs that pay nothing. ~Todd Ruthman

To acquire knowledge, one must study; but to acquire wisdom, one must observe. ~Marilyn vos Savant

Let us not look back in anger, nor forward in fear, but around in awareness. ~James Thurber

If you're not learning while you're earning, you're cheating yourself out of the better portion of your compensation. ~Napoleon Hill

In youth we learn; in age we understand. ~Marie von Ebner-Eschenbach

Watch what people are cynical about, and one can often discover what they lack. ~Harry Emerson Fosdick

Silence is the virtue of fools. ~Francis Bacon

Never tell the truth to people who are not worthy of it. ~Mark Twain

Whatever you believe with emotion becomes your reality. You always act in a manner consistent with your innermost beliefs and convictions. ~Brian Tracey

It is better to ask some of the questions than to know all of the answers. ~James Thurber

Judge a man by his questions rather than his answers. ~Voltaire

The only interesting answers are those which destroy the questions. ~Susan Sontag

You can become blind by seeing each day as a similar one. Each day is a different one, each day brings a miracle of its own. It's just a matter of paying attention to this miracle. ~Paulo Coelho

It is not the answer that enlightens, but the question. ~Eugene Ionesco

Science is just an open-ended discussion that's always going on. ~Hugh Nibley

The only way to prove: enough experience, observation, thinking, personal impression to convince you that it is so. ~ Hugh Nibley

True doctrine, understood, changes attitudes and behavior. The study of the doctrines of the gospel will improve behavior quicker than a study of behavior will improve behavior. ~Boyd K. Packer

Faith is power, obedience the sacrifice, love the means, Christ the reason. ~ Boyd K. Packer

Questions are the creative acts of intelligence. ~Frank Kingdon

To repeat what others have said, requires education; to challenge it, requires brains. ~Mary Pettibone Poole

The uncreative mind can spot wrong answers, but it takes a very creative mind to spot wrong questions. ~Antony Jay

I'm glad I understand that while language is a gift, listening is a responsibility. ~Nikki Giovanni

I never let schooling interfere with my education. ~Mark Twain

Education is the ability to listen to almost anything without losing your temper or your self-confidence. ~Robert Frost

It requires wisdom to understand wisdom: the music is nothing if the audience is deaf. ~Walter Lippmann

I no longer worry about being a brilliant conversationalist. I simply try to be a good listener. I notice that people who do that are usually welcome wherever they go. ~Frank Bettger

Remember: when you talk you only repeat what you already know, but if you listen you may learn something. ~Amish School Saying

It's a mistake to think we listen only with our ears. It's much more important to listen with the mind, the eyes, the body, and the heart. Unless you truly want to understand the other person, you'll never be able to listen. ~Mark Herndon

A child sees everything, looks straight at it, examines it, without any preconceived idea; most people, after they are about eleven or twelve, quite lose this power, they see everything through a few preconceived ideas which hang like a veil between them and the outer world. ~Olive Schreiner

I don't think much of a man who is not wiser today than he was yesterday.~Abraham Lincoln

Wisdom doesn't automatically come with old age. Nothing does - except wrinkles. It's true, some wines improve with age. But only if the grapes were good in the first place. ~Abigail Van Buren

The whole problem with the world is that fools and fanatics are always so certain of themselves, but wiser people so full of doubts. ~Bertrand Russell

Wisdom is what's left after we've run out of personal opinions. ~Cullen Hightower

One's first step in wisdom is to question everything - and one's last is to come to terms with everything. ~Georg Christoph Lichtenberg

The wisest mind has something yet to learn. ~George Santayana

The older I grow the more I distrust the familiar doctrine that age brings wisdom. ~H. L. Mencken

Force without wisdom falls of its own weight. ~Horace

Science is organized knowledge. Wisdom is organized life. ~Immanuel Kant

Men are wise in proportion, not to their experience, but to their capacity for experience. ~James Boswell

It is unwise to be too sure of one's own wisdom. It is healthy to be reminded that the strongest might weaken and the wisest might err. ~Mahatma Gandhi

We don't receive wisdom; we must discover it for ourselves after a journey that no one can take for us or spare us. ~Marcel Proust

To acquire knowledge, one must study; but to acquire wisdom, one must observe. ~Marilyn vos Savant

It is not white hair that engenders wisdom. ~Menander

Those who wish to appear wise among fools, among the wise seem foolish. ~Quintilian,

Like an ability or a muscle, hearing your inner wisdom is strengthened by doing it. ~Robbie Gass

Wisdom outweighs any wealth. ~Sophocles

No man is wise enough by himself. ~Titus Maccius Plautus

Not by age but by capacity is wisdom acquired. ~Titus Maccius Plautus

A wise man can see more from the bottom of a well than a fool can from a mountain top. ~Unknown

Wisdom is not finally tested in the schools, Wisdom cannot be pass'd from one having it to another not having it, Wisdom is of the soul, is not susceptible of proof, is its own proof. ~Walt Whitman

Good people are good because they've come to wisdom through failure. ~William Saroyan

The fool doth think he is wise, but the wise man knows himself to be a fool. ~William Shakespeare

IX. What did She Say?

Life isn't measured by the breaths you take, but by the moments that take your breath away. -Anonymous

The future depends entirely on what each of us does every day. ~Gloria Steinem

We're here for a reason. I believe a bit of the reason is to throw little torches out to lead people through the dark. ~Whoopi Goldberg

It's fun to get together and have something good to eat at least once a day. That's what human life is all about enjoying things. ~Julia Child

Stop worrying about the potholes in the road and celebrate the journey! ~Barbara Hoffman

The most pathetic person in the world is someone who has sight but has no vision. ~Helen Keller

Dreams have only one owner at a time. That's why dreamers are lonely. ~Erma Bombeck

How we spend our days is, of course, how we spend our lives. ~Annie Dillard, The Writing Life

If we would only give, just once, the same amount of reflection to what we want to get out of life that we give to the question of what to do with a two weeks' vacation, we would be startled at our false standards and the aimless procession of our busy days. ~Dorothy Canfield Fisher

I prefer to be a dreamer among the humblest, with visions to be realized, than lord among those without dreams and desires. ~Kahlil Gibran

Some people come into our lives and quickly go. Some stay for a while and leave footprints on our hearts, and we are never the same. ~Flavia Weedn

Living in the moment means letting go of the past and not waiting for the future. It means living your life consciously, aware that each moment you breathe is a gift ~Oprah Winfrey

The real winners in life are the people who look at every situation with an expectation that they can make it work or make it better. ~Barbara Hetcher

In my friend, I find a second self. ~Isabel Norton

Loving can cost a lot, but not loving always costs more. ~Merle Shain

Generosity is not giving me that which I need more than you do, but it is giving me that which you need more than I do. ~Kahlil Gibran

Yesterday is a dream, tomorrow but a vision. But today well lived makes every yesterday a dream of happiness, and every tomorrow a vision of hope. Look well, therefore to this day. ~Sanskrit Proverb

Do what you feel in your heart to be right- for you'll be criticized anyway. You'll be damned if you do, and damned if you don't. ~Eleanor Roosevelt

Yesterday is history. Tomorrow is a mystery. Today is a gift. That's why we call it "The Present."
~Eleanor Roosevelt

one can make you feel inferior without your consent. ~Eleanor Roosevelt

Turn your wounds into wisdom. ~Oprah Winfrey

If I were asked to give what I consider the single most useful bit of advice for all humanity it would be this: Expect trouble as an inevitable part of life and when it comes, hold your head high, look it squarely in eye and say, 'I will be bigger than you. You cannot defeat me.' ~Ann Landers

The best and most beautiful things in the world cannot be seen or even touched. They must be felt with the heart. ~Helen Keller

You never know what happiness a simple act of kindness will bring about. ~Bree Abel

Isolation is aloneness that feels forced upon you, like a punishment. Solitude is aloneness you choose and embrace. I think great things can come out of solitude, out of going to a place where all is quiet except the beating of your heart. ~Jeanne Marie Laskas

Confidence is the sexiest thing a woman can have. It's much sexier than any body part. ~Aimee Mullins

Being a sex symbol has to do with an attitude, not looks. Most men think it's looks; most women know otherwise. ~Kathleen Turner

The cup that is already full cannot have more added to it. In order to receive the further good to which we are entitled, we must give of that which we have. ~Margaret Becker

A bird doesn't sing because it has an answer, it sings because it has a song. ~Maya Angelou

The best index to a person's character is (a) how he treats people who can't do him any good, and (b) how he treats people who can't fight back. ~Abigail van Buren

A sense of humor can help you overlook the unattractive, tolerate the unpleasant, cope with the unexpected, and smile through the unbearable. ~Moshe Waldoks

The easiest way for your children to learn about money is for you not to have any. ~Katharine Whitehorn

Character cannot be developed in ease and quiet. Only through experience of trial and suffering can the soul be strengthened, vision cleared, ambition inspired, and success achieved. ~Helen Keller

Through you I learned how great life can be, how the simple things in life are really the most important and how you treat other people is really all that matters. ~Lisa Scully-O'Grady

The true measure of a man is how he treats someone who can do him absolutely no good. ~Ann Landers

Advice is what we ask for when we already know the answer but wish we didn't. ~Erica Jong

Courage is not the absence of fear, but rather the judgment that something else is more important than fear. ~Ambrose Redmoon

Life shrinks or expands in proportion to one's courage. ~Anais Ninn

To understand the heart and mind of a person, look not at what he has already achieved, but at what he aspires to. ~Khalil Gibran

I postpone death by living, by suffering, by error, by risking, by giving, by losing. ~Anais Ninn

The true secret of giving advice is, after you have honestly given it, to be perfectly indifferent whether it is taken or not, and never persist in trying to set people right. ~Hannah Whitall Smith

I've learned that people will forget what you said, people will forget what you did, but people will never forget how you made them feel. ~Maya Angelou

We have no choice of what color we're born or who our parents are or whether we're rich or poor. What we do have is some choice over what we make of our lives once we're here. ~Mildred D. Taylor

Every day is a new beginning. Treat it that way. Stay away from what might have been, and look at what can be. ~Marsha Petrie Sue

You only live once, but if you do it right, once is enough. ~Mae West

The opposite of love is not hate, it's indifference. ~Elie Wiesel

There may be times when we are powerless to prevent injustice, but there must never be a time when we fail to protest. ~Elie Wiesel

We must always take sides. Neutrality helps the oppressor, never the victim. Silence encourages the tormentor, never the tormented. ~Elie Wiesel

There is divine beauty in learning... To learn means to accept the postulate that life did not begin at my birth. Others have been here before me, and I walk in their footsteps. The books I have read were composed by generations of fathers and sons, mothers and daughters, teachers and disciples. I am the sum total of their experiences, their quests. And so are you. ~Elie Wiesel

Ultimately, the only power to which man should aspire is that which he exercises over himself. ~Elie Wiesel

Not all of us can do great things. But we can do small things with great love. ~Mother Teresa

Pain is inevitable. Suffering is optional. ~M. Kathleen Casey

Without courage, you cannot practice any other virtue. You have to have courage - courage of different kinds: first, intellectual courage, to sort out different values and make up your mind about which is the one which is right for you to follow. You have to have moral courage to stick up to that - no matter what comes in your way, no matter what the obstacle and the opposition is. ~Indira Gandhi

You can't shake hands with a clenched fist. ~Indira Gandhi

You can't underestimate the power of fear. ~Patricia Nixon

Treat yourself to flattering exercise pants and a brightly colored tank. It's a matter of time before science proves that it's more fun to exercise when you look cute. ~Unknown

There's no operation where you can have your anger cut out. But if you work on yourself, as you get better, you'll be more capable of seeing others as flawed human beings. That makes it easier to forgive. ~Robin Quivers

Men are so simple and so ready to obey present necessities, that one who deceives will always find those who allow themselves to be deceived. ~Niccolò Macchiavelli

As long as you don't forgive, who and whatever it is will occupy rent-free space in your mind. ~Isabelle Holland

We can do anything we want to if we stick to it long enough. ~Helen Keller

We plant seeds that will flower as results in our lives, so best to remove the weeds of anger, avarice, envy, and doubt, that peace and abundance may manifest for all. ~Dorothy Day

My philosophy is that not only are you responsible for your life, but doing the best at this moment puts you I the best place for the next moment. ~Oprah Winfrey

Without courage, you cannot practice any other virtue. You have to have courage - courage of different kinds: first, intellectual courage, to sort out different values and make up your mind about which is the one which is right for you to follow. You have to have moral courage to stick up to that - no matter what comes in your way, no matter what the obstacle and the opposition is. ~Indira Gandhi

It is not where you begin, it is where you end that counts. ~Faith Littlefield

Love is like quicksilver in the hand. Leave the fingers open and it stays. Clutch it, and it darts away. ~Dorothy Parker

The problem with people who have no vices is that generally you can be pretty sure they're going to have some pretty annoying virtues. ~Elizabeth Taylor

If grass can grow through cement, love can find you anywhere. ~Cher

A mediocre idea that generates enthusiasm will go farther than a great idea that inspires no one. ~Mary Kay Ash

Adventure is worthwhile in itself. ~Amelia Earhart

Kind words can be short and easy to speak, but their echoes are truly endless. ~Mother Teresa

In helping others, we shall help ourselves, for whatever good we give out completes the circle and comes back to us. ~Flora Edwards

Thank you to all the people in the world who are always 10% kinder than they need to be. That's what really makes the world go round. ~Helen Exley

Plain women know more about men than beautiful ones do. But beautiful women don't need to know about men. It's the men who have to know about beautiful women. ~Katharine Hepburn

It takes two to make a marriage a success and only one a failure. ~Herbert Samuel

If you judge people, you have no time to love them. ~Mother Theresa

Spend the afternoon. You can't take it with you. ~Annie Dillard

Joy is what happens to us when we allow ourselves to recognize how good things really are. ~Marianne Williamson

Was she so loved because her eyes were so beautiful, or were her eyes so beautiful because she was so loved? ~Anzia Yenerska

A good laugh overcomes more difficulties and dissipates more dark clouds than any other one thing. ~Laura Ingalls Wilder

The moment when you first wake up in the morning is the most wonderful of the twenty-four hours. No matter how weary or dreary you may feel, you possess the certainty that, during the day that lies before you, absolutely anything may happen. And the fact that it practically always doesn't, matters not a jot. The possibility is always there. ~Monica Baldwin

Sooner or later we all discover that the important moments in life are not the advertised ones, not the birthdays, the graduations, the weddings, not the great goals achieved. The real milestones are less prepossessing. They come to the door of memory. ~Susan B. Anthony

I got a fortune cookie that said, To remember is to understand. I have never forgotten it. A good judge remembers what it was like to be a lawyer. A good editor remembers being a writer. A good parent remembers what it was like to be a child. ~Anna Quindlen

Money can be translated into the beauty of living. ~Sylvia Porter

You don't get to choose how you're going to die. Or when. You can only decide how you're going to live. Now. ~Joan Baez

The follies which a man regrets most in his life are those which he didn't commit when he had the opportunity. ~Helen Rowland

Each day comes bearing its own gifts. Untie the ribbons. ~Ruth Ann Schabacker

The bitterest tears shed over graves are for words left unsaid and for deeds left undone. ~Harriet Beecher Stowe

That it will never come again
Is what makes life so sweet.
~Emily Dickinson

There are many To-morrows, my Love, my Love, -
There is only one To-day.
~Joaquin Miller

I don't want to get to the end of my life and find that I lived just the length of it. I want to have lived the width of it as well. ~Diane Ackerman

X. What did He Say?

Duty makes us do things well, but love makes us do thing beautifully. ~ Phillips Brooks

God grant me the serenity to accept the things I cannot change, the courage to change the things I can, and the wisdom to know the difference. ~ Reinhold Niebuhr

A happy person is not a person in a certain set of circumstances, but rather a person with a certain set of attitudes. -Hugh Downs

Ideologies separate us. Dreams and anguish bring us together. ~Eugene Ionesco

You cannot teach a man anything; you can only help him find it within himself. ~Galileo

To conquer fear is the beginning of wisdom. ~Bertrand Russell

Do the thing you fear, then the death of fear is certain. ~Brian Tracey

Time is a great teacher, but unfortunately it kills all its pupils. ~Hector Berlioz

Once you face your fear, nothing is ever as hard as you think. ~Olivia Newton-Jonn

No passion so effectually robs the mind of all its powers of acting and reasoning as fear. ~Edmund Burke

Promise me you will always remember you are braver than you believe, stronger than you seem and smarter than you think. ~Christopher Robin to Pooh

The winners in life think constantly in terms of I can, I will, and I am. Losers, on the other hand, concentrate their waking thoughts on what they should have or would have done, or what they can't do. ~Dr. Dennis Waitley

If there were in the world today any large number of people who desired their own happiness more than they desired the unhappiness of others, we could have a paradise in a few years. ~Bertrand Russell

It is hard to believe that a man is telling the truth when you know that you would lie if you were in his place. ~H. L. Mencken

In quarrelling, the truth is always lost. ~Publilius Syrus

The bird of paradise alights only in the hand that does not grasp. ~John Berry

Inaction may be the highest form of action. ~Jerry Brown

Never interrupt your enemy when he is making a mistake. ~Napoleon Bonaparte

Be happy while you're living, for you're a long time dead. ~Scottish Proverb

To always be intending to live a new life, but never find time to set about it - this is as if a man should put off eating and drinking from one day to another till he be starved and destroyed. ~Walter Scott

I still find each day too short for all the thoughts I want to think, all the walks I want to take, all the books I want to read and all the friends I want to see. ~John Burroughs

Never forget that you must die; that death will come sooner than you expect. God has written the letters of death upon your hands. In the inside of your hands you will see the letters M.M. It means "Memento Mori" - remember you must die. ~J. Furniss,

There are a million ways to lose a work day, but not even a single way to get one back. ~Tom DeMarco and Timothy Lister

Obediance is the first law of heaven, and order is the result. ~Rulen S. Wells

You can discover what your enemy fears most by observing the means he uses to frighten you. ~Eric Hoffer

Why fight fury with fury? You'll only blow up the block (or the world). Instead, walk away or stand still and breathe. Give the enemy space and provide yourselves with an opening for mutual understanding. ~Unknown

If we let things terrify us, life will not be worth living. ~Seneca

A tough lesson in life that one has to learn is that not everybody wishes you well. ~Dan Rather

Hatred, The anger of the weak. ~Alphonse Daudet

If you hate a person, you hate something in him that is part of yourself. What isn't part of ourselves doesn't disturb us. ~Hermann Hesse

Always go before our enemies with confidence, otherwise our apparent uneasiness inspires them with greater boldness. ~Napoleon Bonaparte

Nothing brings families together faster than forgiveness. That should make it Step No. 1, but most of us find forgiving hard. We associate it with weakness and losing when, actually, the reverse is true. When you forgive, you gain strength and come out a winner. You break free of control by the other person's actions. ~Dr. Joyce Brothers

Injuries too well remembered cannot heal. ~Benjamin R. Barber

Perhaps there is only one cardinal sin: impatience. Because of impatience we are driven out of Paradise; because of impatience we cannot return. ~Franz Kafka

If you can fix the thing that worries you, then fix it, otherwise don't waste precious time or energy on it. ~Colleen Grant

He who cannot forgive others destroys the bridge over which he himself must pass. ~George Herbert

The things that will destroy us are: politics without principle; pleasure without conscience; wealth without work; knowledge without character; business without morality; science without humanity, and worship without sacrifice. ~Mahatma Gandhi

When the rich wage war it's the poor who die. ~Jean-Paul Sartre

The sin they do two by two they must pay for one by one. ~Rudyard Kipling

Sleep, nature's rest, divine tranquility that brings peace to the mind. ~Ovid

The best words for resolving a disagreement are, 'I could be wrong; I often am.' It's true. ~Brian Tracey

Our body is a machine for living. ~Leo Tolstoy

Durability is part of what makes a great athlete. ~Bill Russell

We understand that you can't transform people who don't have internal drive and desire to create. But we also know it doesn't work to urge people to think outside the box without giving them the tools to climb out. ~Laurie Dunnavant

He who has imagination without learning has wings and no feet. ~Joseph Joubert

Making the simple complicated is commonplace; making the complicated simple, awesomely simple, that's creativity. ~Charles Mingus

Sometimes the best helping hand you can give is a good, firm push. ~Joann Thomas

Don't tell people how to do things. Tell them what to do and let them surprise you with their results. ~George S. Patton

If someone is going down the wrong road, he doesn't need motivation to speed him up. What he needs is education to turn him around. ~Jim Rohn

Advice is like snow; the softer it falls, the longer it dwells upon, and the deeper it sinks into the mind. ~Samuel Taylor Coleridge

Whatever advice you give, keep it short. ~Horace

The influence of each human being on others in this life is a kind of immortality. ~John Quincy Adams

The only way in which one human being can properly attempt to influence another is by encouraging him to think for himself, instead of endeavoring to instill ready made opinions into his head. ~Sir Leslie Stephen

On the whole human beings want to be good, but not too good and not quite all the time. ~George Orwell

When a friend is in trouble, don't annoy him by asking if there is anything you can do. Think up something appropriate and do it. ~Edgar Watson Howe

You cannot reason a person out of a position he did not reason himself into in the first place. ~Jonathan Swift

The truth always turns out to be simpler than you thought. ~Richard Feynman

The truth that many people never understand, until it is too late, is that the more you try to avoid suffering the more you suffer because smaller and more insignificant things begin to torture you in proportion to your fear of being hurt. ~Thomas Merton

It's not a matter of what is true that counts but a matter of what is perceived to be true. ~Henry Kissinger

Once you eliminate the impossible, whatever remains, no matter how improbable, must be the truth. ~Sherlock Holmes

There is one quality which one must possess to win, and that is definiteness of purpose, the knowledge of what one wants, and a burning desire to possess it. ~Napoleon Hill

If you stop searching, you stop living, because then you're dwelling in the past. If you're not reaching forward to any growth or future, you might as well be dead. ~Wynn Bullock

The secret of life is to have a task, something you devote your entire life to, something you bring everything to, every minute of the day for the rest of your life. And the most important thing is, it must be something you cannot possibly do. ~Henry Moore

He only is exempt from failures who makes no efforts. ~Archbishop Richard Whately

Real loss only occurs when you love something more than you love yourself. ~Robin Williams

Death is not the greatest loss in life. The greatest loss is what dies inside us while we live. ~Norman Cousins

Why should I fear death? If I am, death is not. If death is, I am not. Why should I fear that which can only exist when I do not? ~Epicurus

Healthy children will not fear life if their elders have integrity enough not to fear death. ~Erik H. Erikson

The love of money is the root of all evil. ~Paul

To be successful in business, be daring, be first, be different. ~William Marchant

When you do the common things in life in an uncommon way, you will command the attention of the world. ~George Washington Carver

A friendship founded on business is better than a business founded on friendship. ~John D. Rockefeller, Jr.

Every day of our lives we are on the verge of making those slight changes that would make all the difference. ~Mignon McLaughlin

Use your health, even to the point of wearing it out. That is what it is for. Spend all you have before you die; do not outlive yourself. ~George Bernard Shaw

Life happens too fast for you ever to think about it. If you could just persuade people of this, but they insist on amassing information. ~Kurt Vonnegut, Jr.

Here I am trying to live, or rather, I am trying to teach the death within me how to live. ~Jean Cocteau

Whether it's the best of times or the worst of times, it's the only time we've got. ~Art Buchwald

If you woke up breathing, congratulations! You have another chance. ~Andrea Boydston

Life is always walking up to us and saying, "Come on in, the living's fine," and what do we do? Back off and take its picture. ~Russell Baker

Catch, then, oh catch the transient hour;
Improve each moment as it flies!
Life's a short summer, man a flower;
He dies - alas! how soon he dies!
~Samuel Johnson

There's never enough time to do all the nothing you want. ~Bill Watterson, Calvin and Hobbes

Never give a person more power than he can use, for use it he will. ~Cotton Mather

It is easy to be brave from a safe distance. ~Aesop

The fearless are merely fear-less. People who act in spite of their fear are truly brave. ~James A. LaFond-Lewis

Courage is almost a contradiction in terms. It means a strong desire to live taking the form of a readiness to die. ~G. K. Chesterton

Courage is simply the willingness to be afraid and act anyway. ~Robert Anthony

Courage is the art of being the only one who knows you're scared to death. ~Earl Wilson

To face despair and not give in to it, that's courage. ~Ted Koppel

Facts do not cease to exist because they are ignored. ~Aldous Huxley

When you really want something to happen, the whole universe conspires so that your wish comes true. ~Paulo Coelho

There is nothing so strong or safe, in any emergency of life, as simple truth. ~Charles Dickens

It's taken me all my life to understand that it is not necessary to understand everything. ~Rene Coty

Who knows what women can be when they are finally free to become themselves. ~Charles De Gaulle

There is a woman at the beginning of all things. ~Alphonse de Lamartine

All the windows of my heart I open to the day. ~ John Greenleaf Whittier

When you see a woman who can go nowhere without a staff of admirers, it is not so much because they think she is beautiful, it is because she has told them they are handsome. ~Jean Giraudoux

Sometimes your joy is the source of your smile, but sometimes your smile can be the source of your joy. ~Thich Nhat Hanh

The grand essentials of happiness are: something to do, something to love, and something to hope for. ~Allan K. Chalmers

Shall I give you my recipe for happiness? I find everything wonderful and nothing miraculous. ~Norman Douglas

They say a person needs just these things to be truly happy in this world: someone to love, something to do, and something to hope for. ~Tom Bodett

We act as though comfort and luxury were the chief requirements of life, when all that we need to make us really happy is something to be enthusiastic about. ~Charles Kingsley

There are souls in this world which have the gift of finding joy everywhere and of leaving it behind them when they go. ~Frederick Faber

We are meant to express how we feel about life. It's like breathing: Inhale the experiences of life, exhale how you feel about them. We are at our best when we can turn our impressions into expressions. The equation goes like this: Impression without expression equals depression. ~Don Hahn

Medicine, law, business, engineering: these are noble pursuits necessary to sustain life. But poetry, beauty, romance, love ~ these are what we stay alive for. ~Dead Poets Society

If you enjoy the fragrance of a rose, you must accept the thorns which it bears. ~Isaac Hayes

Ideologies separate us. Dreams and anguish bring us together. ~Eugene Ionesco

Some people are making such thorough preparation for rainy days that they aren't enjoying today's sunshine. ~William Feather

I am beginning to learn that it is the sweet, simple things of life which are the real ones after all. ~Laura Ingalls Wilder

Don't try to rewrite what the moving finger has writ, and don't ever look over your shoulder. ~Ogden Nash

Now is no time to think of what you do not have. Think of what you can do with what there is. ~Ernest Hemingway

Far better it is to dare to do mighty things, to win glorious triumphs, even though checkered by failure, than to take rank with those poor spirits who neither enjoy much nor suffer much because they live in the gray twilight that knows not victory nor defeat. ~Theodore Roosevelt

There are two kinds of people who never amount to much: those who cannot do what they are told, and those who can do nothing else. ~Cyrus Curtis

There are 3 types of people in the world...Ones that watch things happen...Ones that make things happen...And ones that wonder what the heck happened! ~Unknown

All people dream, but not equally. Those who dream by night in the dusty recesses of their mind, wake in the morning to find that it was vanity. But the dreamers of the day are dangerous people, for they dream their dreams with open eyes, and make them come true. ~T.E. Lawrence (AKA Lawrence of Arabia)

They who dream by day are cognizant of many things which escape those who dream only by night. ~Edgar Allan Poe

In bed my real love has always been the sleep that rescued me by allowing me to dream. ~Luigi Pirandello

Hold fast to dreams, for if dreams die, life is a broken-winged bird that cannot fly. ~Langston Hughes

There are no great people in this world, only great challenges which ordinary people rise to meet. ~William Frederick Halsy, Jr.

People who are able to do their own thinking should not allow others to do it for them. ~Elbert Hubbard

If you can't see it, before you see it, you'll never see it. ~Dr. Jack Graham

Poor eyes limit your sight; poor vision limits your deeds. ~Franklin Field

Vision without action is a daydream. Action without vision is a nightmare. ~Japanese Proverb

Constant kindness can accomplish much. As the sun makes ice melt, kindness causes misunderstanding, mistrust, and hostility to evaporate. ~Albert Schweitzer

In prosperity, our friends know us; in adversity, we know our friends. ~John Churton Collins

Our character is what we do when we think no one is looking. ~H. Jackson Brown Jr.

Character may be manifested in the greatest moments, but it is made in the small ones. ~Phillips Brooks

Who well lives, long lives; for this age of ours should not be numbered by years, days, and hours. ~Guillaume de Salluste Du Bartas,

You only live once; but if you live it right, once is enough. ~Adam Marshall

Life, if well lived, is long enough. ~Seneca, De Ira

There are but three events in a man's life: birth, life, and death. He is not conscious of being born, he dies in pain, and he forgets to live. ~Jean de la Bruyère

What a folly to dread the thought of throwing away life at once, and yet have no regard to throwing it away by parcels and piecemeal. ~John Howe

Character is doing the right thing when nobody is looking. ~J. C. Watts

A man's character is his fate. ~Heraclitus

Character is simply habit long continued. ~Plutarch

The qualities of a great man are vision, integrity, courage, understanding, the power of articulation, and profundity of character. ~Dwight Eisenhower

The really great man is the man who makes every man feel great. ~G.K. Chesterton

A man's character is determined by how hard he fights for what he believes in. ~Aben Kandel and Warren Duff

It is the heart that makes a man rich. He is rich according to what he is, not according to what he has. ~Henry Ward Beecher

Men do not desire merely to be rich, but to be richer than other men. ~John Stuart Mill

No matter how much madder it may make you, get out of bed forcing a smile. You may not smile because you are cheerful; but if you will force yourself to smile, you'll end up laughing. You will be cheerful because you smile. Repeated experiments prove that when man assumes the facial expressions of a given mental mood, any given mood, then that mental mood itself will follow. ~Kenneth Goode

A sense of humor doesn't mean the ability to tell jokes or make wisecracks. It's a sense of proportion and the courage to smile. It's the ability to take yourself and your problems with a grain of salt, the ability to smile at yourself and the world as well. ~John Luther

If you smile when no one else is around, you really mean it. ~Andy Rooney

The eye only sees what the mind is prepared to comprehend. ~Henri Berson

Those who dance appear insane to those who cannot hear the music. ~Mark Kleiman

Plans get you into things but you must work your way out. ~Will Rogers

Concentrate all your thoughts upon the work at hand. The sun's rays do not burn until brought to a focus. ~Alexander Graham Bell

When written in Chinese, the word 'crisis' is composed of two characters - one represents danger, and the other represents opportunity. ~Saul David Alinsky

Plan your work and work your plan. ~Napoloen Hill

Learn something new. Try something different. Convince yourself that you have no limits. ~Brian Tracey

Never do today what you can put off till tomorrow. Delay may give clearer light as to what is best to be done. ~Aaron Burr

Every man is the architect of his own future. ~Appius Claudius

It wasn't raining when Noah built the ark. ~Howard Ruff

I find it fascinating that most people plan their vacations with better care than they plan their lives. Perhaps that is because escape is easier than change. ~Jim Rohn

The secret of getting ahead is getting started. The secret of getting started is breaking your complex overwhelming tasks into small manageable tasks, and then starting on the first one. ~Mark Twain

If you plan to go the distance, YOU have to do the roadwork. ~Chuck Parker

To do what others cannot do is talent. To do what talent cannot do is genius. ~Will Henry

Talent does what it can; genius does what it must. ~Edward George Bulwer-Lytton

Doing easily what others find difficult is talent; doing what is impossible for talent is genius. ~Henri Frederic Amiel

Don't be vain because you happen to have talent. You are not responsible for that; it was not of your doing. What you do with your talent is what matters. ~Pablo Casals

If you have a talent, use it in every which way possible. Don't hoard it. Don't dole it out like a miser. Spend it lavishly, like a millionaire intent on going broke. ~Brenda Francis

All of us are born for a reason, but all of us don't discover why. Success in life has nothing to do with what you gain in life or accomplish for yourself. It's what you do for others. ~Danny Thomas

Success requires no explanations. Failure permits no alibis. ~Napoleon Hill

If one seeks for success and prepares for failure, he will get the situation he has prepared for. ~Florence Scovel Shinn

If you don't learn to laugh at troubles, you won't have anything to laugh at when you grow old ~Edward W. Howe

We don't stop playing because we grow old; we grow old because we stop playing. ~George Bernard Shaw

You should not confuse your career with your life. ~Dave Barry

Assumptions are the termites of relationships. ~Henry Winkler

We judge ourselves by what we feel capable of doing, while others judge us by what we have already done. ~Longfellow

Remember, people will judge you by your actions, not your intentions. You may have a heart of gold but so does a hard-boiled egg. ~Anonymous

When you're in a good mood, bring up the past. When you're in a bad mood, stick to the present. And when you're not feeling emotional at all, it's time to talk about the future. ~Marilyn Vos Savant

Sometimes when you stand face to face with someone, you cannot see his face. ~Mikhail Gorbachev

The only thing money gives you is the freedom of not worrying about money. ~Johnny Carson

A cynic is a man who knows the price of everything and the value of nothing. ~Oscar Wilde

Nowadays people know the price of everything and the value of nothing. ~Oscar Wilde

Most people fail in life because they major in minor things. ~Anthony Robbins

All the adversity I've had in my life, all my troubles and obstacles, have strengthened me ... You may not realize it when it happens, but a kick in the teeth may be the best thing in the world for you. ~Walt Disney

When one subtracts from life infancy (which is vegetation), sleep, eating and swilling, buttoning and unbuttoning - how much remains of downright existence? ~Lord Byron

Prosperity best discovers vice, but adversity best discovers virtue. ~Francis Bacon

It is better to be feared than loved, if you cannot be both. ~Niccolo Machiavelli

Money, the root of all evil ... but the cure for all sadness. ~Mike Gill

In good times people advertise because they want to; in bad times they advertise because they have to. ~Bruce Barton

Words make you think a thought. Music makes you feel a feeling. A song makes you feel a thought. ~E.Y. Harbug

Sow a thought, and you reap an act; Sow an act, and you reap a habit; Sow a habit, and you reap a character; Sow a character, and you reap a destiny. ~Charles Reade

A kind heart is a fountain of gladness making everything in its vicinity freshen into smiles. ~Washington Irving

Wear a smile and have friends; wear a scowl and have wrinkles. ~George Elliot

He gives little who gives with a frown; he gives much who gives little with a smile. ~The Talmud

It's easy to make a buck. It's a lot tougher to make a difference. ~Tom Brokaw

Maturity begins to grow when you can sense your concern for others outweighing your concern for yourself. ~John Macnaughton

Kindness consists in loving people more than they deserve. ~Joseph Joubert

What wisdom can you find that is greater than kindness? ~Jean-Jacques Rousseau

In truth, the only difference between those who have failed and those who have succeeded lies in the difference of their habits. Good habits are the key to all success. Bad habits are the unlocked door to failure. Thus, the first law I will obey, which precedes all others, is I will form good habits and become their slaves. ~Og Mandino

There are two ways of spreading light - to be the candle or the mirror that reflects it. ~Edith Wharton

What comes from the heart, goes to the heart. ~Samuel Taylor Coleridge

The beauty I am searching for is inside, sometimes hidden by atrocities, that beauty that no eye, no finger will ever be able to perceive, that beauty that time is the only one able to preserve, that beauty that is only released by the heart, the rest slowly but surely perishes and is therefore no good to me at all. ~Philippe Fichot

Know when to tune out. If you listen to too much advice, you may wind up making other people's mistakes. ~Ann Landers

Flatter me, and I may not believe you. Criticize me, and I may not like you. Ignore me, and I may not forgive you. Encourage me, and I will not forget you. ~William Arthur Ward

Get around the right people. Associate with positive, goal-oriented people who encourage and inspire you. ~Brian Tracey

Too many people are thinking of security instead of opportunity. They are more afraid of life than death. ~James F. Byrnes

Anyone who thinks sunshine is happiness has never danced in the rain. ~Author Unknown

Obstacles are those frightful things you see when you take your eyes off your goal. ~Henry Ford

Obstacles are built into every opportunity. You have to be willing to work through them to succeed. ~unknown

Obstacles are necessary for success; victory comes only after many struggles and countless defeats. Yet each struggle, each defeat, sharpens your skills and strengths, your courage and your endurance, your ability and your confidence and thus each obstacle is a comrade-in-arms forcing you to become better or quit. Each rebuff is an opportunity to move forward; turn away from them, avoid them, and you throw away your future. ~Og Mandino

A certain amount of opposition is a great help to a man. Kites rise against, not with, the wind. ~John Neal

Nothing is particularly hard if you divide it into small jobs. ~Henry Ford

Do what you can, with what you have, where you are. ~President Theodore Roosevelt

Become so wrapped up in something that you forget to be afraid. ~Lady Bird Johnson

The saying that knowledge is power is not quite true. Used knowledge is power, and more than power. It is money, and service, and better living for our fellowmen, and a hundred other good things. But mere knowledge, left unused, has no power in it. ~Edward E. Free

These days people seek knowledge, not wisdom. Knowledge is of the past, wisdom is of the future. ~Vernon Cooper

Never mistake knowledge for wisdom. One helps you make a living; the other helps you make a life. ~Sandra Carey

Knowledge comes by taking things apart: analysis. But wisdom comes by putting things together. ~John A. Morrison

Science is organized knowledge. Wisdom is organized life. ~Immanuel Kant

The artist doesn't have time to listen to the critics. The ones who want to be writers read the reviews, the ones who want to write don't have the time to read reviews. ~William Faulkner

In the field of observation, chance favours the prepared mind. ~Louis Pasteur

When we seek to discover the best in others, we somehow bring out the best in ourselves. ~William Arthur Ward

Ordinary riches can be stolen, real riches cannot. In your soul are infinitely precious things that cannot be taken from you. ~Oscar Wilde

Absence makes the heart grow fonder. ~Thomas Haynes Bayly in Isle of Beauty,

Absence extinguishes small passions and increases great ones, as the wind will blow out a candle, and blow in a fire. ~Duc de la Rocherfoucauld

In everyone's life, at some time, our inner fire goes out. It is then burst into flame by an encounter with another human being. We should all be thankful for those people who rekindle the inner spirit. ~Albert Schweitzer

Gratitude is the memory of the heart. ~Jean Baptiste Massieu

Silent gratitude isn't much use to anyone. ~Gladys Berthe Stern

Feeling gratitude and not expressing it is like wrapping a present and not giving it. ~William Arthur Ward

It's simply a matter of doing what you do best and not worrying about what the other fellow is going to do. ~John R. Amos

Like Neanderthals, men prefer to hunt alone or, if in a pack, at the head of it. Women, whether in the field or in a campfire, are collaborative, and when they hunt...they work together. ~Russell Banks

Remember that children, marriages, and flower gardens reflect the kind of care they get. ~H. Jackson Brown

The guys who fear becoming fathers don't understand that fathering is not something perfect men do, but something that perfects the man. ~Frank Pittman

No man can live happily who regards himself alone, who turns everything to his own advantage. You must live for others if you wish to live for yourself. ~SenecaDon't judge each day by the harvest you reap but by the seeds that you plant. ~Robert Louis Stevenson

If you tell the truth, you don't need a long memory. ~Jesse Ventura

Truth does not change according to our ability to stomach it. ~Flannery O'Connor

A good conversationalist is not one who remembers what was said, but says what someone wants to remember. ~John Mason Brown

The true spirit of conversation consists in building on another man's observation, not overturning it. ~Edward G. Bulwer-Lytton

Any intelligent fool can make things bigger, more complex, and more violent. It takes a touch of genius - and a lot of courage - to move in the opposite direction. ~E. F. Schumacher

The fool's mind wanders, the wise mind wonders. ~Patrick J. Mills

Speak softly and carry a big stick. ~Theodore Roosevelt

A loud voice cannot compete with a clear voice, even if it's a whisper. ~Barry Neil Kaufman

Talk low, talk slow, and don't say too much. ~John Wayne

Let thy speech be better than silence, or be silent. ~Dionysius the Elder

Silence is one of the great arts of conversation. ~Marcus Tullius Cicero

You cannot speak that which you do not know. You cannot share that which you do not feel. You cannot translate that which you do not have. And you cannot give that which you do not possess. To give it and to share it, and for it to be effective, you first need to have it. Good communication starts with good preparation. ~Jim Rohn

The most important thing in communication is to hear what isn't being said. ~Peter F. Drucker

Talking is a hydrant in the yard and writing is a faucet upstairs in the house. Opening the first takes the pressure off the second. ~Robert Frost

There are no secrets better kept than the secrets that everybody guesses. ~George Bernard Shaw

Float like a butterfly, sting like a bee. ~Muhammad Ali

A man may die, nations may rise and fall, but an idea lives on. ~John F. Kennedy

You can kill a man but you can't kill an idea. ~Medgar Evers

The best way to have a good idea is to have lots of ideas. ~Linus Pauling

To get your ideas across, use small words, big ideas, and short sentences. ~John H. Patterson

Ideas are the raw material of progress. Everything first takes shape in the form of an idea. But an idea by itself is worth nothing. An idea, like a machine, must have power applied to it before it can accomplish anything. ~B.C. Forbes

Getting an idea is like sitting down on a pin; it should make you jump up and do something. ~E. L. Simpson

Kindness is more than deeds. It is an attitude, an expression, a look, a touch. It is anything that lifts another person. ~C. Neil Strait

You may be sorry that you spoke, sorry you stayed or went, sorry you won or lost, sorry so much was spent. But as you go through life, you'll find ~you're never sorry you were kind. ~Herb Prochnow

Men talk of killing time, while time quietly kills them. ~Dion Boucicault

If you were going to die soon and had only one phone call you could make, who would you call and what would you say? And why are you waiting? ~Stephen Levine

Remember you must die whether you sit about moping all day long or whether on feast days you stretch out in a green field, happy with a bottle of Falernian from your innermost cellar. ~Horace

Time is painted with a lock before, and bald behind, signifying thereby that we must take time by the forelock; for, when it is once past, there is no recalling it. ~Jonathan Swift

Our repugnance to death increases in proportion to our consciousness of having lived in vain. ~William Hazlitt

Those who make the worst use of their time are the first to complain of its shortness. ~Jean de La Bruyère

It's a mere moment in a man's life between an All-Star Game and an Old-timers' Game. ~Vin Scully

When we lose one we love, our bitterest tears are called forth by the memory of hours when we loved not enough. ~Maurice Maeterlinck,

When it comes time to die, make sure all you got to do is die. ~Attributed to Jim Elliot

I think I don't regret a single 'excess' of my responsive youth - I only regret, in my chilled age, certain occasions and possibilities I didn't embrace. ~Henry James

Expect an early death it will keep you busier. ~Martin H. Fischer

The only thing necessary for the triumph of evil is for good men to do nothing. ~Edmund Burke

Man is the only creature who refuses to be what he is. ~Albert Camus

Three things in human life are important: the first is to be kind; the second is to be kind; and the third is to be kind. ~Henry James

People do not lack strength, they lack will. ~Victor Hugo

Idleness, pleasure, what abysses! To do nothing is a dreary course to take, be sure of it. To live idle upon the substance of society! To be useless, that is to say, noxious! This leads straight to the lowest depth of misery. ~Victor Hugo

He never went out without a book under his arm, and he often came back with two. ~Victor Hugo

That in life, which takes the most effort to receive, is more often than not the most worth having..~Chris Sonognini

Mindfulness involves intentionally doing only one thing at a time and making sure I am here for it. ~Jon Kabat-Zinn

Wherever you go, there you are ~Kabat-Zinn

Live your life each day as you would climb a mountain. An occasional glance toward the summit keeps the goal in mind, but many beautiful scenes are to be observed from each new vantage point. Climb slowly, steadily, enjoying each passing moment; and the view from the summit will serve as a fitting climax for the journey. -Harold B. Melchart

A winner is someone who recognizes his God-given talents, works his tail off to develop them into skills, and uses these skills to accomplish his goals. ~Larry Bird

You don't have to burn books to destroy a culture. Just get people to stop reading them. ~Ray Bradbury

Every successful man I have heard of has done the best he could with conditions as he found them, and not waited until next year for better. ~Edgar W. Howe

Things turn out best for those that make the best of the way things turn out. ~Art Linkletter

If you don't have the best of everything, make the best of everything that you have. ~Anonymous

Words that enlighten are more precious than jewels. ~Hazrat Inayat Khan

There is nothing stronger in the world than gentleness. ~Han Suyin

Nobody, on their deathbed, ever said, “I wish I'd spent more time at the office.” ~ Stephen Covey

The amount you give isn't important. What matters is what that amount represents in terms of your life. ~Jim Rohn

Give to the world the best you have, and the best will come back to you. ~Madeline S. Bridges

Nothing you do for children is ever wasted. They seem not to notice us, hovering, averting our eyes, and they seldom offer thanks, but what we do for them is never wasted. ~Garrison Keillor

Solitude is the human condition in which I keep myself company. Loneliness comes about when I am alone without being able to split up into the two-in-one, without being able to keep myself company. ~Hannah Arendt

Talents are best nurtured in solitude: character is best formed in the stormy billows of the world. ~Goethe

To be persuasive, one must be believable. To be believable, we must be credible. To be credible, we must be truthful. ~Edward R. Murrow

The chief lesson I have learned in a long life is that the only way you can make a man trustworthy is by trusting him; and the surest way to make him untrustworthy is to distrust him and show your distrust. ~-Henry L. Stimson

Dreams are essential to life. ~Anais Nin

I would I could stand on a busy corner, hat in hand, and beg people to throw me all their wasted hours. ~Bernard Berenson

I have spent my days stringing and unstringing my instrument, while the song I came to sing remains unsung. ~Tagore

Many people die with their music still in them. Why is this so? Too often it is because they are always getting ready to live. Before they know it, time runs out. ~Oliver Wendell Holmes

Contemplation often makes life miserable. We should act more, think less, and stop watching ourselves live. ~Nicolas de Chamfort

I held a moment in my hand, brilliant as a star, fragile as a flower, a tiny sliver of one hour. I dripped it carelessly, Ah! I didn't know, I held opportunity. ~Hazel Lee

We die daily. Happy those who daily come to life as well. ~George MacDonald

Gather ye rose-buds while ye may
Old Time is still a-flying;
And this same flower that smiles today,
Tomorrow will be dying.
~Robert Herrick

Most of us spend our lives as if we had another one in the bank. ~Ben Irwin

If you wait, all that happens is that you get older. ~Larry McMurtry, Some Can Whistle

In theory one is aware that the earth revolves, but in practice one does not perceive it, the ground upon which one treads seems not to move, and one can live undisturbed. So it is with Time in one's life. ~Marcel Proust

If I could only remember that the days were, not bricks to be laid row on row, to be built into a solid house, where one might dwell in safety and peace, but only food for the fires of the heart. ~Edmund Wilson

The only thing that will stop you from fufilling your dreams is you. ~Tom Bradley

We won't always know whose lives we touched and made better for our having cared, because actions can sometimes have unforeseen ramifications. What's important is that you do care and you act. ~Charlotte Lunsford

Children need models more than they need critics. ~Joseph Joubert

No gift is too small to give, nor too simple to receive, if it's chosen with thoughtfulness and given with love. ~Unknown

The difficulty with marriage is that we fall in love with a personality, but must live with a character. ~Peter Devries

A person's character is what it is. It's a little like a marriage ~ only without the option of divorce. You can work on it and try to make it better, but basically you have to take the bitter with the sweet. ~Hendrick Hertzberg

I only want to love once, but I want to love everybody for the rest of my life. ~Lauren Ford

All that glitters is not gold ~John Dryden

Nothing is sadder than having worldly standards without worldly means. ~Van Wyck Brooks

If you have wit, use it to please and not to hurt: you may shine like the sun in the temperate zones without scorching. ~Lord Chesterfield

Tact is the knack of making a point without making an enemy. ~Isaac Newton

People who know little are usually great talkers, while men who know much say little. ~Jean Jacques Rousseau

I may not have gone where I intended to go, but I think I have ended up where I intended to be. ~Douglas Adams

The future is not some place we are going, but one we are creating. The paths to it are not found but made, and the activity of making them changes both the maker and the destination. ~John Schaar

It may make a difference to all eternity whether we do right or wrong today. ~James Freeman Clark

One very important aspect of motivation is the willingness to stop and to look at things that no one else has bothered to look at. This simple process of focusing on things that are normally taken for granted is a powerful source of creativity. ~Edward de Bono

Simplicity is the essence of the great, the true, and the beautiful in art. ~George Sand

Simplicity is the ultimate sophistication. ~Leonardo da Vinci

Ability is important, dependability is critical! ~Alexander Lockheart

It's all right letting yourself go as long as you can let yourself back. ~Mick Jagger

Nothing is more effective than sincere, accurate praise, and nothing is more lame than a cookie-cutter compliment. ~Bill Walsh

It is discouraging how many people are shocked by honesty and how few by deceit. ~Noël Coward

Fear not the path of truth for the lack of people walking on it. ~Arab proverb

In an age of universal deceit, telling the truth is a revolutionary act. ~George Orwell

When I tell the truth, it is not for the sake of convincing those who do not know it, but for the sake of defending those that do. ~William Blake

If you tell the truth you don't have to remember anything. ~Mark Twain

We do not stop playing because we're old. We grow old because we stop playing. ~ Anonymous

A real friend is one who walks in when the rest of the world walks out. ~Walter Winchell

Many people die with their music still in them. Why is this so? Too often it is because they are always getting ready to live. Before they know it, time runs out. ~Oliver Wendell Holmes Jr.

There'll be two dates on your tombstone and all your friends will read 'em. But all that's gonna matter is that little dash between 'em ~Kevin Welch

Develop your willpower so that you can make yourself do what you should do, when you should do it, whether you feel like it or not. ~Brian Tracy

Life moves pretty fast. If you don't stop every now and then and look around, you could miss it. ~Ferris Beuler

If you want your life to be a magnificent story, then begin by realizing that you are the author and every day you have the opportunity to write a new page. ~Mark Houlahan

Be who you are and say what you feel because those who mind don't matter and those who matter don't mind. ~Theodor Seuss Geisel, Dr. Seuss

If a man does his best, what else is there? ~General George S. Patton

We must be willing to let go of the life we have planned, so as to have the life that is waiting for us. ~E.M. Forster

To live is the rarest thing in the world. Most people exist, that is all. ~Oscar Wilde

Be nice to nerds. Chances are you'll end up working for one. ~Bill Gates

Logic will get you from A to Z; imagination will get you everywhere. ~Albert Einstein

I have always imagined that Paradise will be some kind of library. ~Jorge Luis Borges

I have had a great many troubles in my life, and most never happened. Mark Twain

The man who follows the crowd will usually get no further than the crowd. The man who walks alone is likely to find himself in places no one has ever been.-Alan Ashley-Pitt

To a brave man, good and bad luck are like his left and right hand. He uses both.~Benito Mussolini

You are today where your thoughts have brought you. You will be tomorrow where your thoughts take you. ~James Allen

We become what we think about. ~Napoleon Hill

I have no right to say or do anything that diminishes a man in his own eyes, what matters is not what I think of him, but what he thinks of himself. Hurting a man in his dignity is a crime. ~Exupry

Age is an issue of mind over matter. If you don't mind, it doesn't matter. ~Mark Twain

It is what you read when you don't have to that determines what you will be when you can't help it. ~Oscar Wilde

I find television very educating. Every time somebody turns on the set, I go into the other room and read a book. ~Groucho Marx

Be Yourself; everyone else is already taken. ~Oscar Wilde

Why did the achievers overcome problems while thousands are overwhelmed by theirs? They refused to hold on to the common excuses for failure. They turned their stumbling blocks into stepping stones. They realized that they couldn't determine every circumstance in life but they could determine their choice of attitude towards every circumstance. ~John Maxwell

Love is that condition in which the happiness of another person is essential to your own. ~Robert A. Heinlein

If the world were merely seductive, that would be easy. If it were merely challenging, that would be no problem. But I arise in the morning torn between a desire to improve the world and a desire to enjoy the world. This makes it hard to plan the day. ~E.B. White

A writer who waits for ideal conditions under which to work will die without putting a word to paper. ~E.B. White

God doesn't expect less of us as we grow and learn he expects more. Expect more out of people and yourself. ~ Chris Sonognini

Ones affirmation of attitude will make it a reality. ~ Chris Sonognini

Every man dies. Not every man really lives.n~Braveheart

Absence makes the heart grow fonder. ~Thomas Haynes Bayly

Do not take life too seriously. You will never get out of it alive. ~Elbert Hubbard

As you grow older, you'll find the only things you regret are the things you didn't do. ~Zachary Scott

Why always "not yet"? Do flowers in spring say "not yet"? ~Norman Douglas

Life is not lost by dying; life is lost minute by minute, day by dragging day, in all the thousand small uncaring ways. ~Stephen Vincent Benét

There is no cure for birth and death save to enjoy the interval. ~George Santayana

For a long time it had seemed to me that life was about to begin - real life. But there was always some obstacle in the way. Something to be got through first, some unfinished business, time still to be served, a debt to be paid. Then life would begin. At last it dawned on me that these obstacles were my life. ~Fr. Alfred D'Souza

Why must conversions always come so late? Why do people always apologize to corpses? ~David Brin

To change one's life: Start immediately. Do it flamboyantly. No exceptions. ~William James

A man that is young in years may be old in hours, if he has lost no time. ~Francis Bacon, Essays

You will never find time for anything. If you want time you must make it. ~Charles Buxton

Death twitches my ear."Live," he says, "I am coming."~Virgil

He has spent all his life in letting down empty buckets into empty wells; and he is frittering away his age in trying to draw them up again. ~Sydney Smith

Fear not that life shall come to an end, but rather fear that it shall never have a beginning. ~John Henry Cardinal Newman

We cannot waste time. We can only waste ourselves. ~George M. Adams

Half our life is spent trying to find something to do with the time we have rushed through life trying to save. ~Will Rogers

Men talk of killing time, while time quietly kills them. ~Dion Boucicault

Time is what we want most, but. what we use worst. ~Willaim Penn

Many a man gets weary of clamping down on his rough impulses, which if given occasional release would encourage the living of life with salt in it, in place of dust. ~Henry S. Haskins

The future has a way of arriving unannounced. ~George F. Will

We do not do what we want and yet we are responsible for what we are - that is the fact. ~Jean Paul Sartre

Time goes, you say? Ah no!
Alas, Time stays, we go.
~Henry Austin Dobson

Regret for the things we did can be tempered by time; it is regret for the things we did not do that is inconsolable. ~Sydney J. Harris

Waste your money and you're only out of money, but waste your time and you've lost a part of your life. ~Michael Leboeuf

A clever person solves a problem. A wise person avoids it." ~Albert Einstein

I believe that imagination is stronger than knowledge. That myth is more potent than history. That dreams are more powerful than facts. That hope always triumphs over experience. That laughter is the only cure for grief. And I believe that love is stronger than death. ~Robert Fulghum

There may be luck in getting a job, but there's no luck in keeping it. ~J. Ogden Armour

Luck is when opportunity meets preparation. ~Denzel Washington

You hit homeruns not by chance but by preparation. ~Roger Maris

Spectacular achievement is always preceded by spectacular preparation. ~Robert Schuller

Luck is being ready for the chance. ~J. Frank Doble

What we do today, right now, Will have an accumulated effect on all our tomorrows. ~Alexandra Stoddard

Someone is sitting in the shade today because someone planted a tree a long time ago. ~Warren Buffet

The butterfly counts not months but moments, and has time enough. ~Rabindranath Tagore

The question for each man is not what he would do if he had the means, time, influence, and educational advantages, but what he will do with the things he has. ~Hamilton

May you live all the days of your life. ~Jonathan Swift

Live as you will wish to have lived when you are dying. ~Christian Furchtegott Gellert

Life is not long, and too much of it must not pass in idle deliberation how it shall be spent. ~Samuel Johnson

The swift years slip and slide adown the steep;
The slow years pass; neither will come again.
~William Sharp

The proper function of man is to live, not to exist. I shall not waste my days in trying to prolong them. ~Jack London

Life is what happens to us while we are making other plans. ~Thomas La Mance

The value of moments, when cast up, is immense, if well employed; if thrown away, their loss is irrevocable. ~Lord Chesterfield

PART IV

I. UNKNOWN

When you were born, you cried and the world rejoiced. Live your life in such a manner that when you die the world cries and you rejoice. ~Indian Saying

We're fools whether we dance or not, so we might as well dance. ~Japanese Proverb

No man is quick enough to enjoy life to the full. ~Spanish Proverb

Better to be a lion for one day than a hundred years as a maggot.~ English Proverb

The tragedy of life is not that it ends so soon, but that we wait so long to begin it.

The inherent virtue of procrastination is always having plans for tomorrow.

They say procrastination is the source of all my sorrows. Unfortunately I don't know what that big words means. I'll look it up tomorrow.

It isn't procrastination if you put it off right away.

If they took the last minute away from me, I wouldn't get anything done.

A healthy attitude is contagious but don't wait to catch it from others. Be a carrier.

Although at the moment they may be equal in their lack of a real answer, the man who replies I'll find out, is much more valuable to his employer, his neighbor, and to himself than the man who replies I don't know.

Attitudes are contagious. Are yours worth catching?

His mother asked him why he said that when the day was anything but beautiful. Mother, said he, with rare wisdom, never judge a day by its weather.

I can alter my life by altering the attitude of my mind.

Take charge of your attitude. Don't let someone else choose it for you.

The control center of your life is your attitude.

Although fate presents the circumstances, how you react depends on your character.

A person shows what he is by what he does with what he has.

A person who aims at nothing is sure to hit it.

A smile is a window on your face to show your heart is at home.

A word of encouragement during a failure is worth more than an hour of praise after success.

Achieving starts with believing.

Every day is an opportunity to make a new happy ending.

Action speaks louder than words - but not nearly as often.

All the so-called "secrets of success" will not work unless you do.

Don't ever save anything for a special occasion. Being alive is the special occasion.

An important project was begun, a bishop quoted an ancient sage as saying, "If our thoughts and hopes are elsewhere, it is impossible for us to set our faces steadily toward the work required of us."

Anything unattempted remains impossible.

True courage is not the absence of fear; rather it is the taking of action in spite of the fear.

At a distance from home a man is judged by what he means.

By working faithfully eight hours a day, you may eventually get to be boss and work 12 hours a day.

Character is a diamond that scratches every other stone.

Character is a victory, not a gift.

Character, like a kettle, once mended, always requires repairs.

Encouraged people achieve the best; dominated people achieve second best; neglected people achieve the least.

Even a mosquito doesn't get a slap on the back until it starts to work.

Failure is not the worst thing in the world. The very worst is not to try.

When your life flashes before your eyes, make sure you've got plenty to watch.

Failure is the path of least persistence.

Goals that are not written down are just wishes.

God does not ask about our ability, but our availability.

God gives us dreams a size too big so that we can grow in them.

God put me on earth to accomplish a certain number of things. Right now I am so far behind I will never die!

God put me on Earth to accomplish a certain number of things. Right now I'm so far behind I will never die!

Ideas are funny little things. They don't work unless you do.

If you aim at nothing, you'll hit it every time.

If you chase two rabbits, both will escape.

If you don't climb the mountain, you can't view the plain.

If you wish to live wisely, ignore sayings including this one.

If you're not living on the edge, you're taking up too much space.

In order to succeed, you must first be willing to fail.

In the darkest hour the soul is replenished and given strength to continue and endure.

It is wise to keep in mind that no success or failure is necessarily final.

It's not the work that's hard, it's the discipline.

Never be afraid to do something new. Remember, amateurs built the ark; professionals built the titanic.

No duty is more urgent than that of returning thanks.

One of the most difficult things to give away is kindness; it usually comes back to you.

Only those who do nothing make no mistakes.

Remember that great love and great achievements involve great risk.

Present your family and friends with their eulogies now - they won't be able to hear how much you love them and appreciate them from inside the coffin.

Reputation is the shell a man discards when he leaves life for immortality. His character he takes with him.

Reputation is what the world thinks a man is; character is what he really is.

Self-determination is fine but needs to be tempered with self-control.

Some people grin and bear it; others smile and do it.

Sometimes we are limited more by attitude than by opportunities.

The harder you fall, the higher you bounce.

The only real failure in life is the failure to try.

The true gentleman does not preach his beliefs until he does so by his actions.

Tis better to buy a small bouquet
And give to your friend this very day,
Than a bushel of roses white and red
To lay on his coffin after he's dead.

Warning: Dates in Calendar are closer than they appear.

II. Short Stories, Poems, and Longer Quotes

RISK

To laugh is to risk appearing the fool.

To weep is to risk appearing sentimental.

To reach out for another is to risk involvement.

To expose your feelings is to risk exposing your true self.

To place your ideas, your dreams before a crowd is to risk their loss.

To Love is to risk not being loved in return.

To live is to risk dying.

To hope it to risk despair.

To try it to risk failure.

But risks must be taken because thegreatest hazard in life is to risk nothing.

The person who risks nothing ... has nothing ... is nothing.

You may avoid suffering and sorrow,

but you simply cannot learn, feel, change, grow, love...live.

Chained by your certitudes, you are a slave; you have forfeited freedom.

Only a person who risks is free.

~ Ralph Waldo Emerson

WHAT IS SUCCESS?

To laugh often and much;

To win the respect of intelligent people
and the affection of children;

To earn the appreciation of honest critics
and endure the betrayal of false friends;

To appreciate beauty;
To find the best in others;

To leave the world a bit better, whether by
a healthy child, a garden patch
or a redeemed social condition;

To know even one life has breathed
easier because you have lived;

This is to have succeeded.

~Ralph Waldo Emerson ~

Tomorrow Is Not Promised!

Sometimes people come into your life and you know right away that they were meant to be there. They serve some sort of purpose, teach you a lesson, or help you figure out who you are and who you want to be. You never know why these people may be: your neighbor, child, long lost friend, lover, or even a complete stranger. Who, when you lock eyes with you know at that very moment, that they will affect your life is some profound way.

And sometimes things happen to you and at the time they seem painful and unfair, but in reflection you realize that without overcoming those obstacles you would have never realized your potential strength, willpower, or heart.

Everything happens for a reason. Nothing happens by chance or by means of good or bad luck. Illness, injury, love, lost moments of true greatness and sheer stupidity all occur to test the limits of your soul.

Without these small test, whether they be events, illnesses or relationships, life would be like a smoothly paved straight flat road to nowhere, safe and comfortable, but dull and utterly pointless. The people you meet who affect your life and the successes and downfalls you experience create who you are, and even the bad experiences can be learned from, in fact, they are probably the poignant and the important ones. If someone hurts you, betrays you or breaks your heart, forgive them, for they have helped you learn about trust and the importance of being cautious to whom you open your heart too. If someone loves you, love them back unconditionally, not only because they love you, but because they are teaching you to love and opening your heart and eyes to things you would have never seen or felt without them. Make every day count. Appreciate every moment and take from it everything that you possibly can, for you may never be able to experience it again. Talk to people you have never talked to before, and actually listen, let yourself fall in love, break free and set your sights high! Hold your head up, because you have every right too. Tell yourself you are a great individual and believe in yourself, for if you don't believe in yourself, no one else will believe in you either. Create your own life and then go out and live in it! " Live Each Day As If It Were Your Last! Tomorrow Is Never Promised."

-Promise Yourself-

To be so strong that nothing can disturb your peace of mind.
To talk health, happiness, and prosperity to every person you meet.
To make all your friends feel that there is something in them.
To look at the sunny side of everything and make your optimism come true.
To think only the best, to work only for the best and expect only the best.
To be just as enthusiastic about the success of others as you are about your own.
To forget the mistakes of the past and press on to the greater achievements of the future.
To give so much time to the improvement of yourself that you have no time to criticize others.
To be too large for worry, too noble for anger, too strong for fear, and too happy to permit the presence of trouble
-The Optimist Clubs Of America-

The Race

attributed to Dr. D.H. "Dee" Groberg

Whenever I start to hang my head in front of failure's face,
my downward fall is broken by the memory of a race.
A children's race, young boys, young men; how I remember well,
excitement sure, but also fear, it wasn't hard to tell.
They all lined up so full of hope, each thought to win that race
or tie for first, or if not that, at least take second place.
Their parents watched from off the side, each cheering for their son,
and each boy hoped to show his folks that he would be the one.

The whistle blew and off they flew, like chariots of fire,
to win, to be the hero there, was each young boy's desire.
One boy in particular, whose dad was in the crowd,
was running in the lead and thought "My dad will be so proud."
But as he speeded down the field and crossed a shallow dip,
the little boy who thought he'd win, lost his step and slipped.
Trying hard to catch himself, his arms flew everyplace,
and midst the laughter of the crowd he fell flat on his face.
As he fell, his hope fell too; he couldn't win it now.
Humiliated, he just wished to disappear somehow.

But as he fell his dad stood up and showed his anxious face,
which to the boy so clearly said, "Get up and win that race!"
He quickly rose, no damage done, behind a bit that's all,
and ran with all his mind and might to make up for his fall.
So anxious to restore himself, to catch up and to win,
his mind went faster than his legs. He slipped and fell again.
He wished that he had quit before with only one disgrace.
"I'm hopeless as a runner now, I shouldn't try to race."

But through the laughing crowd he searched and found his father's
face
with a steady look that said again, "Get up and win that race!"
So he jumped up to try again, ten yards behind the last.

"If I'm to gain those yards," he thought, "I've got to run real fast!"
Exceeding everything he had, he regained eight, then ten...
but trying hard to catch the lead, he slipped and fell again.
Defeat! He lay there silently. A tear dropped from his eye.
"There's no sense running anymore! Three strikes I'm out! Why try?
I've lost, so what's the use?" he thought. "I'll live with my disgrace."
But then he thought about his dad, who soon he'd have to face.

"Get up," an echo sounded low, "you haven't lost at all,
for all you have to do to win is rise each time you fall.
Get up!" the echo urged him on, "Get up and take your place!
You were not meant for failure here! Get up and win that race!"
So, up he rose to run once more, refusing to forfeit,
and he resolved that win or lose, at least he wouldn't quit.
So far behind the others now, the most he'd ever been,
still he gave it all he had and ran like he could win.
Three times he'd fallen stumbling, three times he rose again.
Too far behind to hope to win, he still ran to the end.

They cheered another boy who crossed the line and won first place,
head high and proud and happy -- no falling, no disgrace.
But, when the fallen youngster crossed the line, in last place,
the crowd gave him a greater cheer for finishing the race.
And even though he came in last with head bowed low, unproud,
you would have thought he'd won the race, to listen to the crowd.
And to his dad he sadly said, "I didn't do so well."
"To me, you won," his father said. "You rose each time you fell."

And now when things seem dark and bleak and difficult to face,
the memory of that little boy helps me in my own race.
For all of life is like that race, with ups and downs and all.
And all you have to do to win is rise each time you fall.
And when depression and despair shout loudly in my face,
another voice within me says, "Get up and win that race!"

Eleanor Roosevelt wrote:

Many people will walk in and out of your life,
But only true friends will leave footprints in your heart.
To handle yourself, use your head;
To handle others, use your heart.

Great minds discuss ideas;
Average minds discuss events;
Small minds discuss people.
He who loses money, loses much;
He, who loses a friend, loses much more;
He, who loses faith, loses all.

Beautiful young people are accidents of nature,
But beautiful old people are works of art.

Learn from the mistakes of others.
You can't live long enough to make them all yourself.

"Myself"

"I have to live with myself, and so

I want to be fit for myself to know,

I want to be able, as days go by,

Always to look myself straight in the eye;

I don't want to stand, with the setting sun,

And hate myself for the things I've done.

I don't want to keep on a closet shelf

A lot of secrets about myself,

And fool myself, as I come and go,

Into thinking that nobody else will know

The kind of man that I really am;

I don't want to dress up myself in sham.

"I want to go out with my head erect

I want to deserve all men's respect;

But here in the struggle for fame and pelf,

I want to be able to like myself.

I don't want to look at myself and know

That I'm bluster and bluff and empty show.

"I never can hide myself from me;

I see what others can never see;

I know what others may never know;

I never can fool myself, and so,

Whatever happens, I want to be

Self-respecting and conscience free."

Edgar A. Guest

"Albert Einstein's Rules of Work"

1) Out of clutter, find simplicity.

2) From discord, find harmony.

3) In the middle of difficulty lies opportunity."

~Albert Einstein

THE INTERVIEW WITH GOD

I dreamed I had an interview with God.

“So you would like to interview me?” God asked.

“If you have the time” I said.

God smiled. “My time is eternity.”
“What questions do you have in mind for me?”

“What surprises you most about humankind?”

God answered...
“That they get bored with childhood,
they rush to grow up, and then
long to be children again.”

“That they lose their health to make money...
and then lose their money to restore their health.”

“That by thinking anxiously about the future,
they forget the present,
such that they live in neither
the present nor the future.”

"That they live as if they will never die,
and die as though they had never lived.”

God’s hand took mine
and we were silent for a while.

And then I asked...
“As a parent, what are some of life’s lessons
you want your children to learn?”

“To learn they cannot make anyone

love them. All they can do
is let themselves be loved."

"To learn that it is not good
to compare themselves to others."

"To learn to forgive
by practicing forgiveness."

"To learn that it only takes a few seconds
to open profound wounds in those they love,
and it can take many years to heal them."

"To learn that a rich person
is not one who has the most,
but is one who needs the least."

"To learn that there are people
who love them dearly,
but simply have not yet learned
how to express or show their feelings."

"To learn that two people can
look at the same thing
and see it differently."

"To learn that it is not enough that they
forgive one another, but they must also forgive themselves."

"Thank you for your time," I said humbly.

"Is there anything else
you would like your children to know?"

God smiled and said,
"Just know that I am here... always."

~Author Unknown

The EDGE

Come to the edge,
He said.
We can't, it's too high.

Come to the edge,
He said.
We can't, we might fall.

Come to the edge,
He said.
And they came
And he pushed
And they flew!

~an English poet

Fear

Precarious: “Willpower?”

Willpower: “Yes, Precarious?”

Precarious: “I wish our parents didn’t name me so. I fear they named me all to well. I wish I had a name like yours,”

Willpower: “You know Precarious my named hasn’t always been Willpower?”

Precarious: “It hasn’t? I thought that was your real name?”

Willpower: “Oh it was. I thought are parents named me well also. You see Precarious; they called me Scared when I was younger. And believe me I was scared of everything. I didn’t dare to try and accomplish anything.”

Precarious: “Yeah right! You scared? You’re not scared of anything. You can do anything you put your mind to.”

Willpower: “Your right and your wrong. I feel fear all of the time, but I don’t let it rule me. I’ve learned to rule my fear. There is only two ways you can look at everything; to be scared or not to be scared.”

Precarious: “What do you mean Will?”

Willpower: “What I mean is that our parents named us this way for a reason. They want to teach us a lesson, but it took me a long time to figure that out. Our parents had a valuable lesson in mind when they named us. The best thing they could teach us!”

Precarious: “Really? What lesson is that?”

Willpower: “That our minds, Precarious…, either make us, or they break us.”

Precarious: “So what you’re saying Will is that the only reason I feel so uncertain of things is because of what is in my mind.”

Willpower: “Exactly!”

Precarious: “So you’re saying I can overcome my fears, if in my mind, I don’t let it overpower me.”

Willpower: “Exactly! Fear doesn’t come from without, but from within.”

Precarious: “I think I understand! When did your name change?”

Willpower: “I never told you about the day I met Fear?”

Precarious: “What? You met Fear? He is awfully frightening. You never told me about that, you must have been very scared.”

Willpower: “I was very scared. It was a time of life—much like yours—where I was fed up with who I thought I was.”

Precarious: “What happened?”

Scared: “It was early one morning I was walking on the trail not far from our house, thinking of all of the things I was scared of, when I bumped into Fear. I fell on the ground and looked up. Fear was grinning down at me.”

Fear: “Watch where you’re going boy.” He yelled at me.

Scared: Boy? I’m over 20; I’m not a boy I thought to myself. And what is he doing walking on this side of the path. “Sorry sir, I didn’t mean too.”

Fear: He laughed. “Boy why don’t you run off home to your mommy?”

Scared: I didn't want to go home. I wanted to finish my walk. "Yes sir, your absolutely right, it's late I should be getting home." It wasn't late at all.

Fear: He laughed "You coward. You live up to your name well."

Scared: I turned and started walking the other way. I could still hear him laughing. Then something snapped inside me. I had enough. I didn't want to be scared anymore, I screamed to myself. I walked back up to Fear.

Precarious: "You did, you did! What did you say?"

Scared: Well, first, Fear had this hideous look on his face. (I about tuned around and left) but then he said to me,

Fear: "Was there something you wanted to say Scared."

Scared: I met his menacing eyes with a fire of my own. And for the first time in my life, I felt utterly calm. I had no fear what so ever. "I don't fear you."

Fear: He screeched. "You don't fear me?" He laughed. "Scared doesn't fear me, impossible!"

Scared: I calmly stared at Fear. He stopped laughing, and again, for the first time in my life I recognized fear for what it was, and for the first time it wasn't me that was the one radiating fear. I could see fear in Fears eyes.

Fear: "You fear me boy." He said without much resolve.

Willpower: "No… I don't."

Precarious: "You did?"

Willpower: "Yes, and I also said, you have a choice Fear. I can go around you, over you, or under you. And since I prefer not to go under or over, for obvious reasons, I will go through you!" I said in a cold voice.

Precarious: "Wow! What did he do?"

Willpower: "What did he do? He ran off because he knew there was a train on his path this day, and nothing was going to stop it."

Precarious: "Do you think I will ever meet Fear?"

Willpower: "I'm sure you will, very sure! I never answered your question when I got named."

Precarious: "Oh yeah! So who named you?"

Willpower: "Well, when I got home Dad was at the door. Determination looked me straight in the eye and said, 'welcome home Willpower.'"

Precarious: Some months later Precarious came rushing home yelling for Willpower. He was met at the door by his mom. Adamant looked him in the eye, and with pride said, "welcome home Valiant."

Valiant: "Willpower I have a new name! Finally!"

Willpower: "I'm very proud of you Valiant. What did you learn from Fear?"

Valiant: "There is only one way to look at fear, with 'Adamant' 'Determination', and knowing nothing short of death 'Will' stop you."

Willpower: "Very good, Valiant."

~by Chris Sonognini

Put The Glass Down

There is a story about a professor who is presenting a lecture on stress management to his students. He raised a glass of water and asked the class, "How heavy do you think this glass of water is?" The students guessed about 6 ounces. "It doesn't matter what the absolute weight is. It depends on how long you hold it," the professor replied. "If I hold it for a minute, it is ok. If I hold it for an hour, my arm will start to ache. If I hold it for a day, you will have to call an ambulance. It is the exact same weight, but the longer I hold it, the heavier it becomes."

If you carry your burdens all the time, sooner or later, you will not be able to carry on, the burden will be too heavy. What you have to do is put the glass down and rest for a while before holding it up again. You have to put down the burdens from time to time, so that you can be refreshed and able to carry on. Whatever burden you are carrying on your shoulders, let it down. Take a rest. If you must, you can pick it up again later when you have rested. Rest and relax

~Unknown source

The Painting

A wealthy man and his son loved to collect rare works of art. They had everything in their collection, from Picasso to Raphael. They would often sit together and admire the great works of art. When the Viet Nam conflict broke out, the son went to war. He was very courageous and died in battle while rescuing another soldier.

The father was notified and grieved deeply for his only son. About a month later, just before Christmas, there was a knock at the door. A young man stood at the door with a large package in his hands. He said, "Sir, you don't know me, but I am the soldier for whom your son gave his life. He saved many lives that day, and he was carrying me to safety when a bullet struck him in the heart and he died instantly. He often talked about you, and your love for art."

The young man held out his package. "I know this isn't much. I'm not really a great artist, but I think your son would have wanted you to have this."

The father opened the package. It was a portrait of his son, painted by the young man. He stared in awe at the way the soldier had captured the personality of his son in the painting.

The father was so drawn to the eyes that his own eyes welled up with tears. He thanked the young man and offered to pay him for the picture.

"Oh, no sir, I could never repay what your son did for me. It's a gift."

The father hung the portrait over his mantle. Every time visitors came to his home he took them to see the portrait of his son before he showed them any of the other great works he had collected.

The man died a few months later. There was to be a great auction of his paintings. Many influential people gathered, excited over seeing the great paintings and having an opportunity to purchase one for their collection. On the platform sat the painting of the son. The auctioneer pounded his gavel. We will start the bidding with this picture of the son.

Who will bid for this picture?" There was silence. Then a voice in the back of the room shouted, "We want to see the famous paintings. Skip this one."

But the auctioneer persisted. "Will someone bid for this painting? Who will start the bidding? $100, $200?"

Another voice shouted angrily. "We didn't come to see this painting. We came to see the Van Gogh's, the Rembrandts. Get on with the real bids!"

But still the auctioneer continued. The son! The son! Who'll take the son?

Finally, a voice came from the very back of the room. It was the longtime gardener of the man and his son.

"I'll give $10 for the painting." Being a poor man, it was all he could afford.

"We have $10, who will bid $20?"

"Give it to him for $10. Let's see the masters."

"$10 is the bid, won't someone bid $20?"

The crowd was becoming angry. They didn't want the picture of the son. They wanted the more worthy investments for their collections. The auctioneer pounded the gavel. "Going once, twice, SOLD for $10!"

A man sitting on the second row shouted, "Now let's get on with the collection!"

The auctioneer laid down his gavel. "I'm sorry, the auction is over."

"What about the paintings?"

"I am sorry. When I was called to conduct this auction, I was told of a secret stipulation in the will. I was not allowed to reveal that stipulation until this time. Only the painting of the son would be auctioned.

Whoever bought that painting would inherit the entire estate, including the paintings. The man who took the son gets every thing!"

God gave His son 2,000 years ago to die on a cruel cross. Much like the auctioneer, His message today is, "The son, the son, who'll take the son?" Because, you see, whoever takes the Son gets everything.

~Author Not Known

"Today"

Today is here. I will begin with a smile and will resolve to be agreeable. I will not criticize. I refuse to waste the valuable time, God has given me.

Today has one thing in which I know I am equal with all others — Time! All of us draw the same salary in seconds, minutes, and hours.

Today I will not waste time because the minutes I wasted yesterday areas lost as a vanished thought!

Today I refuse to spend my time worrying about what might happen. I am going to spend my time making things happen!

Today I am determined to improve myself. For tomorrow I may be needed and I must not be found lacking.

Today I begin by doing and not wasting my time. In one week I will be miles beyond the person I am today.

Today I will not imagine what I would do if things were different. They are not different. I will make a success with what I have.

Today I will act towards other people as though this might be my last day on earth. I will not wait for tomorrow. Tomorrow never comes.

Today I will stop saying, “If I make time,” “If I find time,” “If I had time,” for I never will find time for anything—if I want time, I MUST MAKE TIME.

~Unknown

I Have a Dream

I say to you today, my friends, so even though we face the difficulties of today and tomorrow, I still have a dream. It is a dream deeply rooted in the American dream.

I have a dream that one day this nation will rise up and live out the true meaning of its creed: "We hold these truths to be self-evident: that all men are created equal."

I have a dream that one day on the red hills of Georgia the sons of former slaves and the sons of former slave owners will be able to sit down together at the table of brotherhood.

I have a dream that one day even the state of Mississippi, a state sweltering with the heat of injustice, sweltering with the heat of oppression, will be transformed into an oasis of freedom and justice.

I have a dream that my four little children will one day live in a nation where they will not be judged by the color of their skin but by the content of their character.

I have a dream today.

I have a dream that one day, down in Alabama, with its vicious racists, with its governor having his lips dripping with the words of interposition and nullification; one day right there in Alabama, little black boys and black girls will be able to join hands with little white boys and white girls as sisters and brothers.

I have a dream today.

I have a dream that one day every valley shall be exalted, every hill and mountain shall be made low, the rough places will be made plain, and the crooked places will be made straight, and the glory of the Lord shall be revealed, and all flesh shall see it together.

This is our hope. This is the faith that I go back to the South with. With this faith we will be able to hew out of the mountain of despair a stone of hope. With this faith we will be able to transform the jangling discords of our nation into a beautiful symphony of brotherhood. With this faith we will be able to work together, to pray together, to struggle together, to go to jail together, to stand up for freedom together, knowing that we will be free one day."

~Martin Luther King Jr.

Friends

A simple friend can stand by you when you are right,
but a real friend will stand by you even when you are wrong.
A simple friend identifies himself when he calls.
A real friend doesn't have to.

A simple friend opens a conversation with a full news bulletin on his life.
A real friend says, "What's new with you?"

A simple friend thinks the problems you whine about are recent.
A real friend says, "You've been whining about the same thing for 14 years.
Get off your duff and do something about it."

A simple friend has never seen you cry.
A real friend has shoulders soggy from your tears.

A simple friend doesn't know your parents' first names.
A real friend has their phone numbers in his address book.

A simple friend brings a bottle of wine to your party.
A real friend comes early to help you cook and stays late to help you clean.

A simple friend hates it when you call after he has gone to bed.
A real friend asks you why you took so long to call.

A simple friend seeks to talk with you about your problems.
A real friend seeks to help you with your problems.

A simple friend wonders about your romantic history.
A real friend could blackmail you with it.

A simple friend, when visiting, acts like a guest.
Real friend opens your refrigerator and helps himself/herself.

A simple friend thinks the friendship is over when you have an argument.
A real friend knows that it's not a friendship until after you've had a fight.

A simple friend expects you to always be there for them.
A real friend expects to always be there for you!

~ Author Unknown

Friends

Love starts with a smile, grows with a kiss, and ends with a tear.

Don't cry over anyone who won't cry over you.

Good friends are hard to find, harder to leave, and impossible to forget.

You can only go as far as you push.

Actions speak louder than words.

The hardest thing to do is watch the one you love, love somebody else.

Don't let the past hold you back, you're missing the good stuff.

Life's short. If you don't look around once in a while you might miss it.

A BEST FRIEND is like a four leaf clover, HARD TO FIND and LUCKY TO HAVE.

Some people make the world SPECIAL just by being in it.

BEST FRIENDS are the siblings God forgot to give us.

When it hurts to look back, and you're scared to look ahead, you can look beside you and your BEST FRIEND will be there.

TRUE FRIENDSHIP NEVER ENDS. Friends are FOREVER.

Good friends are like stars....You don't always see them, but you know they are always there.

Don't frown. You never know who is falling in love with your smile.

What do you do when the only person who can make you stop crying is the person who made you cry?

Nobody is perfect until you fall in love with them.

Everything is okay in the end. If it's not okay, then it's not the end.

Most people walk in and out of your life, but only friends leave footprints in your heart.

~ Author Unknown

Dalai Lama

1. Take into account that great love and great achievements involve great risk.

2. When you lose, don't lose the lesson.

3. Follow the three Rs: Respect for self, Respect for others and Responsibility for all your actions.

4. Remember that not getting what you want is sometimes a wonderful stroke of luck.

5. Learn the rules so you know how to break them properly.

6. Don't let a little dispute injure a great friendship.

7. When you realize you've made a mistake, take immediate steps to correct it.

8. Spend some time alone every day.

9. Open your arms to change, but don't let go of your values.

10. Remember that silence is sometimes the best answer.

11. Live a good, honorable life. Then when you get older and think back, you'll be able to enjoy it a second time.

12. A loving atmosphere in your home is the foundation for your life.

13. In disagreements with loved ones deal only with the current situation. Don't bring up the past.

14. Share your knowledge. It's a way to achieve immortality.

15. Be gentle with the earth.

16. Once a year, go someplace you've never been before.

17. Remember that the best relationship is one in which your love for each other exceeds your need for each other.

18. Judge your success by what you had to give up in order to get it.

19. Approach love and cooking with reckless abandon. I also know that dreams really do come true and you have my Best Wishes and my best efforts in those.

Things to Remember

1. No one can ruin your day without YOUR permission.
2. Most people will be about as happy, as they decide to be.
3. Others can stop you temporarily, but only you can do it permanently.
4. Whatever you are willing to put up with is exactly what you will have.
5. Success stops when you do.
6. When your ship comes in....make sure you are willing to unload it.
7. You will never have it all together.
8. Life is a journey....not a destination. Enjoy the trip!
9. The biggest lie on the planet: When I get what I want, I will be happy.
10. The best way to escape your problem is to solve it.
11. I've learned that ultimately, 'takers' lose and 'givers' win.
12. Life's precious moments don't have value, unless they are shared.
13. If you don't start, it's certain you won't arrive.
14. We often fear the thing we want the most.
15. He or she who laughs....lasts.
16. Yesterday was the deadline for all complaints.
17. Look for opportunities....not guarantees.
18. Life is what's coming.... not what was.
19. Success is getting up one more time.
20. Now is the most interesting time of all.
21. When things go wrong.....don't go with them.

~Unknown Author

Unleashing the Dormant Spirit

F. ENZIO BUSCHE

Embrace this day with an enthusiastic welcome, no matter how it looks. The covenant with God to which you are true enables you to become enlightened by him, and nothing is impossible for you.

* When you are physically sick, tired, or in despair, steer your thoughts away from yourself and direct them, in gratitude and love, toward God.

* In your life there have to be challenges. They will either bring you closer to God and therefore make you stronger, or they can destroy you. But you make the decision of which road you take.

* First and foremost, you are a spirit child of God. If you neglect to feed your spirit, you will reap unhappiness. Don't permit anything to detract you from this awareness.

* You cannot communicate with God unless you have first sacrificed your self-oriented natural man and have brought yourself into the lower levels of meekness, to become acceptable for the Light of Christ.

* Put all frustrations, hurt feelings, and grumblings into the perspective of your eternal hope. Light will flow into your soul.

* Pause to ponder the suffering Christ felt in the Garden of Gethsemane. In the awareness of the depth of gratitude for him, you appreciate every opportunity to show your love for him by diligently serving in his Church.

* God knows that you are not perfect. As you suffer about your imperfections, he will give you comfort and suggestions of where to improve.

* God knows better than you what you need. He always attempts to speak to you. Listen, and follow the uncomfortable suggestions that he makes to us ~everything will fall into its place.

* Avoid any fear like your worst enemy, but magnify your fear about the consequences of sin.

* When you cannot love someone, look into that person's eyes long enough to find the hidden rudiments of the child of God in him.

* Never judge anyone. When you accept this, you will be freed. In the case of your own children or subordinates, where you have the responsibility to judge, help them to become their own judges.

* If someone hurts you so much that your feelings seem to choke you, forgive and you will be free again.

* Avoid at all cost any pessimistic, negative, or criticizing thoughts. If you cannot cut them out, they will do you harm. On the road toward salvation, let questions arise but never doubts. If something is wrong, God will give you clarity but never doubts.

* Avoid rush and haste and uncontrolled words. Divine light develops in places of peace and quiet. Be aware of that as you enter places of worship.

* Be not so much concerned about what you do, but do what you do with all your heart, might, and strength. In thoroughness is satisfaction.

* You want to be good and to do good. That is commendable. But the greatest achievement that can be reached in our lives is to be under the complete influence of the Holy Ghost. Then he will teach us what is really good and necessary to do.

* The pain of sacrifice lasts only one moment. It is the fear of the pain of sacrifice that makes you hesitate to do it.

* Be grateful for every opportunity to serve. It helps you more than those you serve.

* And finally, when you are compelled to give up something or when things that are dear to you are withdrawn from you, know that this is your lesson to be learned right now. But know also that, as you are learning this lesson, God wants to give you something better.

"From Beyond Me"

Time is like the wind
That comes in the morning
With a barely palpable caress of the cheek
Rising to a comfortable caress
In its measured passage of the day
Until it rises a sudden gale
Revealing the irrevocability of its power
Trembling our browning leaves
And blowing them to our finality.
~Phillip Pulfrey, , www.originals.net

Time wears all his locks before;
Take thy hold upon his forehead;
When he flies, he turns no more,
And behind his scalp is naked.
~Robert Southwell

Our time consumes like smoke, and posts away;
Nor can we treasure up a month or day:
The sand within the transitory glass
Doth haste, and so our silent minutes pass.
~Rowland Watkyns

EMERSON

All mankind love a lover.

Hitch your wagon to a star.

Shallow men believe in luck.

We boil at different degrees.

Every hero becomes a bore at last.

Men are better than their theology.

Thou art to me a delicious torment.

To be great is to be misunderstood.

Nothing can bring you peace but yourself.

Self-trust is the first secret of success.

Every sweet has its sour; every evil its good.

Whoso would be a man must be a non-conformist.

A creative economy is the fuel of magnificence.

The faith that stands on authority is not faith.

In skating over thin ice our safety is our speed.

Made in the USA
San Bernardino, CA
18 December 2012